PASSION, GUTS & LEADERSHIP

PRAISE FOR PASSION, GUTS & LEADERSHIP

I laughed, I cried, and then I laughed and cried some more...! What a journey. And what a life story that has shaped Deborah into the strong, gutsy, and successful woman she is today. This book is jam-packed with strategies, tips and advice that have been learned by living a life, both personally and professionally, with courage, resilience and authenticity. Kudos to Deborah for sharing such great insights and life's adventures.

Dr Loretta Piazza
Former principal, mentor, coach, podcaster

Deborah Patterson is a leader determined to improve pedagogical practice for our students, through guiding, mentoring and nurturing school leaders and staff. A household name in principal networks, she possesses courage, integrity, honesty and humility. Her many years in education, wisdom and expertise are invaluable and have seen so many schools, staff and students reap the benefits of her guidance, my own included.

Melissa Lozanovski
Principal

Having been a colleague of Deborah Patterson over the past 15 years, I have been continually impressed with her strong and authentic leadership style. Her traits of courage, strength, honesty and integrity shine through whilst creating a leadership framework that is driven to succeed in obtaining the goals set out on a clearly defined vision for all stakeholders. I would strongly recommend any leader to read her publications.

Jason McBean
Principal

Deborah Patterson is an inspiring mentor. She conveys her depth of knowledge and experience in creative and engaging ways that motivates me as a principal. She is passionate about education and mentoring and has been a great support and inspiration.

Maria Giordana
Principal

PASSION, GUTS & LEADERSHIP

An A–Z for the unconventional educational leader

Deborah Patterson

Copyright © Deborah Patterson 2022

All rights reserved. No part of this book may be reproduced or transmitted in any form or by any means, electronic or mechanical, including photocopying, recording or by any information storage and retrieval system, without prior permission in writing from the publisher.

Published by Amba Press
Melbourne, Australia
www.ambapress.com.au

Editor—Francesca Hoban Ryan
Cover designer—Tess McCabe

ISBN: 9781922607362 (pbk)
ISBN: 9781922607379 (ebk)

A catalogue record for this book is available from the National Library of Australia.

CONTENTS

Introduction   1

A
Accountability   9
Agility   11
Alcoholism   12
Alignment model   13
Arrogance   15
Attitude   16

B
Balance   17
Best version of yourself   18
Body language   18
Bosses   19
Budgeting   22
Bullying   23

C
Calm in a crisis... He has a gun!	25
Coaching	28
Confidence	30
Curiosity	32

D
Decluttering	33
Department of Education	34
Do it every day	35
Do not cross the line	36

E
Eating well	39
Energy and stamina	40
Enthusiasm	41
Eyes on the prize	41

F
Fair, firm and fun	43
Fools	45
Foresight, oversight and insight	46

G
Goals	49
Guts, courage, grit and grunt	51

H
Happiness	53
Head, heart and hand	55
Humour and laughter	55

I
Interviews	57

J
Journeys and pathways	65
Juggling	66

K
Kindness	69
Knowing what to know	70
Knowledge and skills	71

L
Ladders	73
Leader as anthropologist	77
Leadership styles	78
Learning process	82
Listening	85

M
Mental models	87
Mentoring	90
Motivation	92

N
Negotiables and non-negotiables	95
Network and network more	96
No!	98

O
Openness	99
Optimism	100
Organisation	101

P
Passion	103
Planning	105
Persistence	105
Principal	106
Prioritising	108
Purpose	110

Q
Quirky	111
Quotes	112

R
3 Rs: Reset, refocus and repurpose	115
Relationships	117
Resume	118
Roles and responsibilities	120
Routines	120

S
Self-care	125
Staff	127
Students	128
Suicide	134

T
Teachers	135
Tough times	136
Toxicity	138

U
Under pressure	143
Unsatisfactory performance	144

V
Values	147
Vancouver	148
Vision	149
Voice	150
Volunteering	152

W
Wardrobe	153
Women	153
Wonder moments	155

X
Crossing things off your list	157

Y
Yellow sunflowers	161

Z
Zones	163
Zzz... Sleep and sync	164
Conclusion	167

INTRODUCTION

One of the most amazing gifts that leadership offers is the opportunity to wake up every day and choose how you want to make a difference. The choices and decisions you make will determine the type of leader you will be. Live in congruence with your beliefs and values. Be honest in your intentions and actions. Learn from your failures and reflect upon your mistakes so that you do not repeat them. Your actions create a legacy that reflects who you are.

You're here because you want more than your typical educator. You want to build an environment that brings out the highest potential of everyone in it. That starts with you! How does a leader navigate the chartered waters of school transformation? How can you leverage your experiences and the lessons you will learn? What icebergs should you be looking for as you steer your ship along the course to its eventual destination? What warning signs will tell you that you are pushing yourself or others too hard? How will you know when your head is not aligned with your body and you are out of balance? When should a leader lead, manage or step aside? Which tools should you be using for school improvement? What tangible and intangible evidence should you be looking for to prove traction, impact and growth?

My purpose in writing this book is to provide teachers, educators and principals with a collection of tips, tools and strategies from my 46 years in education and 22 in leadership. It is my belief that all students deserve the best possible versions of their educators, so that they can become the best versions of themselves and look forward to a future full of opportunities.

I am not your conventional leader. In fact, I am quite the opposite. But what or who is a conventional leader? I spent most of my career learning on the job, making humongous mistakes, picking myself up and putting one foot in front of the other. I wished that I had a crystal ball to save me heartache, sleepless nights and anxiety. Trying to do it all while ignoring the warning signs led to inordinate stress. I might not have suffered breast cancer, a stroke and a tumour on my thyroid if I had tuned in to what my body was trying to tell me. Being lifelong learners, we make discoveries as we go along. But what if we understood more of what we needed to know ahead of time? Would that help us be better versions of ourselves, better teachers and better leaders? Knowledge can save your life. After a long career as an educator and now as a mentor to other principals, I offer here my best advice. I hope that my trials and tribulations can ease your path as a leader.

MY STORY

My parents met in 1955 outside Young and Jackson's Hotel on the corner of Flinders and Swanston Streets in Melbourne. It was a chance meeting. My mother was with a girlfriend, and they were both 17 and dressed in their finest. She noticed a tall, dark and handsome man in a naval uniform. He was also with a friend, and they all smiled politely and stopped to talk. As my father was on a mission to get inside the hotel for a cold VB or Fosters beer, he said to my mother after some small talk and flirting that he'd see her later. My mother, who was no fool, replied, 'Give me your watch as security. That way I know you'll meet me afterwards.' That is how their love story began.

I am the second of four siblings. My brother was born 11 months before me and for one month we are 'twins' of the same age. A second brother born after me sadly died at six weeks, and my two sisters came along a couple of years later. Our family moved constantly: my father was a Chief Petty Officer in the Royal Australian Navy and was sent to various ports around Australia. We lived a transient life mostly in naval housing estates and rental properties. I became accustomed to packing my few possessions and relocating to a new house, flat, hotel or barracks. Life was an adventure, as my father always said. Where will we land this time? Who will we meet? It wasn't all fun: my brother and I were often bashed up and bullied at our schools. I was usually known as the new girl who looked different to everyone. Being poor, we always wore second-hand uniforms and hand-knitted jumpers. Yes, our life was anything but typical.

My father Kevin was a scholarly young man who had to leave school in his teens to go out to work when his father died. He was a champion swimmer and athlete and still holds the fastest backstroke record at his school. He trained as a boilermaker and welder, entering the navy at 18. He rose to the rank of Chief Petty Officer servicing the engine rooms of large naval ships. After leaving the navy he worked in several jobs with heavy machinery. My mother Judith was an only child born to parents known as card sharks who played the local poker circuit in St Kilda. Judith often slept on couches in the houses where my grandparents would play their nightly card games. She would be carried, wrapped in a blanket as she slept, to their car in the early hours of the morning.

My maternal grandmother Hope Evelyn (Nannie to us grandkids) was born in the Victorian town of Maldon. She was small in stature and had her hair done in a beehive every Friday at the hairdressers. Nannie loved a brandy. She worked as a maître d' at the Chevron Hotel in St Kilda Road, and this was where she met my grandfather George.

George was a taxi driver. He was an orphan, and we believe his parents came from Germany. We tried tracing his heritage but the orphanage had lost his details, so we never discovered anything about his family history. George was a big, loud, proud man who had a reputation for being tough and was known by many as a man you did not mess with. When you got into his taxi you knew he was the boss, and you did not talk back to him.

I was born in 1956 in the Arncliffe Hospital, New South Wales, and spent my earliest years in the Sydney suburb of Kogarah. My family then flew up to Darwin where I went to kindergarten and was the only white girl in my class. After a couple of years in Darwin my father decided to leave the navy, so we relocated to Clayton in Victoria. It was the only house we ever owned. Sometime later my grandparents and parents sold their houses and moved to Rochester in regional Victoria. We lived in the Victoria Hotel in Rochester for a couple of years while my parents and grandparents co-managed the pub. There I attended St Joseph's Ladies College.

After a bust-up between my parents and grandparents, we returned to Melbourne and settled in Sandringham where my brother and I went to Hampton High School. I remember being teased because we could not afford the uniform. I spent most of my lunchtimes in the library hiding from the 'mean girls'. My parents and grandparents eventually made up, so we returned to Rochester. I could not go back to St Joseph's because my parents had not paid any fees, so my brother and I went to Rochester High School. I went to three different schools in Form 1 (now known as Year 7). I started making three cookery aprons, a requirement in my Sewing and Home Economics classes, and did not finish one! At the end of Form 1 we moved back to Melbourne and settled in Brunswick.

When I was in Year 11, we mysteriously left that house in Brunswick in a 'midnight flee' and moved to the 20th floor of the Fitzroy high-rise Housing Commission flats. I was later to learn that a 'midnight flee' is done when you are so far behind in your weekly rent that you need to leave a place quickly in the secret of the night. Our new address was 201/140 Brunswick Street Fitzroy. Try writing that as your address! Living in the high-rise flats was a total culture shock.

Alcoholism was an issue with both my parents, and this significantly affected our relationships and careers. Dad loved a beer, mum loved a wine and together they drank every day of the week. I was brought up in a household where fights on Friday and Saturday night were common occurrences. I learnt to retreat to my room, the local library or the park to seek peace and refuge. Many times, I would come home to find my father trying to lift my mother over the railing of the 20th floor of the Fitzroy Housing Commission flats. Dad, I would call out, stop it! Both had been drinking excessively throughout the day. I would separate them and take them inside our flat. To settle them down and distract them from killing each other, I would make my father some pikelets and my mother some cucumber or onion sandwiches with lots of butter, salt and pepper. After an hour or two they both fell asleep, and peace was restored. Mental illness and addiction do not go away; they lie low only to resurface later—in my family's case, later meant every weekend.

In 1973 my peers nominated me as captain of Brunswick High School, on a day when I was sick and did not attend school. The next day everyone told me the news and remarked on how happy I must be. Happy, I thought to myself, I'm devastated! My stomach did a complete 360-degree turn. School captains were supposed to be smart; they were bright, educated, well-respected students who were high achievers and got great scores in their subjects. I kept thinking that I would be the only school captain in the history of Brunswick High School to fail their High School Certificate. To my despair, I won the student election. Everyone was happy except me. All year I carried with me the pressure of making sure I passed my subjects with high scores. I did pass in the end, but it meant 3-4 hours of study every single night, something I would not wish upon any student let alone a school captain.

That year I was also named captain of the Under-16 Victorian netball team. That was a captaincy role that I was happy about. Not bad for a girl who lived in the Fitzroy Housing Commission flats and had to travel by tram to and from netball training, playing games during the week and every Saturday. My parents could not afford my tracksuit, blazer, shoes or uniform so my coach pitched in and paid for everything. I am indebted to him and remember him fondly. His act of kindness also inspired me later in life when I volunteered with the YMCA and the Victorian Association for the Care and Resettlement of Offenders (VACRO).

I worked part-time at Coles Collingwood on Friday nights after school and Saturday mornings before racing off to play and umpire netball at Royal Park in Parkville. I learnt how to schedule school, study, work and high-level sport. Being organised and disciplined allowed me to get through my final year with the goal of university or teachers' college at the end. Did I have a social life? No! When I gave my address to a boy I had met, he laughed and said goodbye. My peers thought I was nuts for living in the flats. Juggling my many roles throughout that year would teach me some lifelong skills: how to set a goal, work hard and celebrate my success regardless of what others thought.

In the meantime, the strain of life was breaking our family apart. Alcohol, drugs, street violence and a culture of uncertainty devastated our once close-knit group, and my siblings and I went different ways as a result of our environment. I lived in the flats for three demoralising years until I won a studentship that enabled me to train as a teacher.

I was the only one in the family to go to teachers' college and later university. I moved into the Warwillah Hostel in St Kilda Road, a residence for female students at Melbourne State College. My time in Fitzroy had prepared me well for communal living by teaching me to be street-smart. My love life started to look up now that I was no longer living in Fitzroy!

At Warwillah I met new friends: Margie, Cas and Jacqui. A year later, we all decided to rent a house in Brunswick. The rent for a four-bedroom terrace house was only $38 per week, and we were right on the train line and close to pubs and the city. In our first year of teaching, Margie and I moved into another house. I married at the end of 1977 and moved to Coburg with my new husband Des.

Des and I met at a football match in 1976. I did not like going to football clubs on Saturday nights, and I especially did not want to go to the Carlton Football Club this particular night. I was with a group of friends. We were in the disco room when one of my friends headed off to the toilet. Next thing I knew, a bump to my left shoulder caused me to spill my drink. I turned around, ready to go mad as I had lost most of my Tia Maria, Coke and cream drink (very expensive in those days!), and was completely surprised. Expecting to see my friend, I said, 'So you're back from the toilet.' When I turned to my left, I noticed that it was a complete stranger. He replied 'Yes,' with an Irish accent and a cheeky grin. 'Yes, I am back,' he said. He was much taller than me, had the deepest of blue eyes, a handlebar moustache, and what an accent! He bought my friend group a round of drinks and later asked me to dance. We sneaked off for a kiss after a few dances, which was something I had never done before. Four weeks later to the day and in the same room, the stranger with an Irish accent and handlebar moustache asked me to marry him. Eighteen months on we had our wedding reception in that very room.

You never know when you are going to meet the love of your life, and I discovered that I was a sucker for an Irish accent. I later learnt that my hero had fallen asleep in the toilets for three hours prior to meeting me. He had come straight off night shift and gone to the game with little sleep, then washed his face, combed his hair and bumped into me. The rest is history. During our stay in our first house in Coburg, we were robbed four times in one year. We decided to move to a flat in Reservoir. After four years of marriage we had saved a deposit for a house in Bundoora, which cost a grand total of $37,750. We are still living in the same house, which has undergone many renovations after 40 years. I learnt how to manage my money, adjust to living in a three-bedroom house in suburbia and build a sound foundation for a family. I loved having real neighbours, going to the local parks, shops and schools, and being part of a community.

I began my teaching career at Brunswick South West Primary School in 1977 and went on to teach at several other primary schools: Coburg, Campbellfield Heights and Keon Park. I was Assistant Principal at Greenbrook, Acting Principal at Panton Hill, Principal at Templestowe Valley, and finally ended my career as Principal at Mill Park Heights. In a six-month seconded position, I was also Senior Project Officer for Maribyrnong College sports academy in 2006.

My work kept me constantly busy, but the stress did not do me good. I learnt in 2002 that I had breast cancer. I could hear the car horns in the distance and the cheerful sounds of the outdoor celebrations from the window as I lay in my hospital bed on the balmy New Year's Eve night heralding in 2003. I remember my uneasy feeling of loneliness, fear and uncertainty. I promised myself that night that if I survived my cancer, I would change my purpose in life. I aimed to choose a new direction and make my existence more meaningful. Armed with a positive mindset and steely determination to make a difference, I began to plan my future.

After the saga of breast cancer, chemotherapy and radiation I had to jump yet another health hurdle when I had a stroke in 2019. Again it felt like I was being tested. This time I would need to do something different. I left full-time work as a principal to pursue my next career as a mentor and author. I had dodged two life-threatening bullets and was not prepared to take another risk. I am now living the dream: a career that lets me use my strengths, do something that I love and work to my own timetable.

I have always been passionate about taking on leadership roles in education. I quickly learnt that I needed more than passion to get through some of the challenges you will read about in this book. I needed guts! Guts to put up with the harshest of situations, the overwhelming workload, the long hours, the difficult and uncompromising people, the life-threatening challenges and the health issues. I saw people behave inappropriately and ruin their lives, relationships and careers. I am sharing some of my stories to equip you with the necessary tools, tips, skills and strategies to avoid these pitfalls and succeed in your leadership journey.

ACCOUNTABILITY

I felt a heavy burden of accountability throughout my professional life as a teacher and a principal. As some of my staff would say to me, 'That's why you get paid the big bucks!' They were right. When you are a leader, your salary comes with the expectation that you are accountable 24/7.

As a teacher or a principal, you are expected to work toward a desired outcome and not simply complete a set of tasks. You must plan strategically and follow through on all goals and targets until the outcome is achieved. Holding staff accountable was a constant challenge for me during my principalship. Assigning responsibility to others for their behaviour and actions is so important in education: you are part of a larger system that affects staff, students, parents and the wider school community.

It is critical to outsource or delegate areas of responsibility, but remember: the leader is responsible for what goes on, and it is their head that rolls if something goes wrong. I was responsible for ensuring fiscal integrity, ethical fundraising processes, strategic risk-management guidelines, sustainable leadership and sound employment practices. It is important for you to take responsibility for what you do with data and to use it effectively. A leader must have appropriate measures and records in place to be able to demonstrate compliance.

Tips for accountability

1. Be honest when mistakes are made and discuss them openly
2. Involve all stakeholders in goal-setting processes
3. Share transparent expectations about everyone's purpose and part to play
4. Make sure physical resources align with set goals
5. Provide honest, open and regular feedback
6. Adhere to all guidelines and recommendations from the Department of Education
7. Live the values of honesty and integrity
8. Do all the training necessary for you to understand your obligations
9. Seek legal advice when needed
10. Always play by the book when you are new in a position of responsibility
11. Never take risks with other people's money
12. Never fiddle with or fudge the numbers
13. Always keep a paper trail for important decisions
14. Join a professional association or union

I like to think that my staff considered me resilient, resourceful and honest. Fun, fair and firm! I wanted my staff to know I would follow through on the things I said I would do. Having a happy, positive attitude towards life and its challenges works best for leaders and everyone else in a school or organisation.

I did stuff up several times in my working career, and I learnt from those experiences. Most of my mistakes related to a lack of accountability. Having an understanding boss who spoke to me respectfully and pointed out my faults or the expectation of my role enabled me to learn and grow. I spoke to my staff when they made errors in a similar way: respectfully and honestly. I wanted the culture at all my schools to be one of support and guidance, where everyone reinforced the value of accountability and knew exactly what was expected of them. If you do not cultivate this type of open culture, then it is assumed by some that they can get away with anything. Unfortunately, this mindset can permeate an entire school.

The most important thing for leaders to remember is not to make mistakes with money or numbers. We are held accountable for all spending, revenue and expenditure and must answer to all forms of fiscal management. Being charged with misappropriation of government funds is not a good outcome! Luckily this did not happen to me. I was fortunate to have great business managers who knew how to plan, allocate, track and run compliant reports. Besides, I would not look good in a green jumpsuit!

I did have to deal with several staff who showed a lack of accountability for foolish behaviour: turning up late, making racial jokes, not following through with tasks, speaking disrespectfully to other staff, not completing reports on time, not being a good team member, lying about where they were and doing something that they should not have been doing. These were some of the most challenging discussions I had as a leader. Some went well and some did not. I would reflect later on what had worked and what had not, making sure to seek feedback and do better next time. Good, better, best!

If a leader turns their head and does not hold people accountable, then bad behaviours will continue. Having tough conversations is a short-term pain, but the steps that you agree to put in place can benefit all parties and enable everyone to stay on track and grow as professionals. These collective and agreed measures improve workplace culture.

AGILITY

Being agile requires flexibility and adaptability. In education, we encounter new issues and circumstances every single day. Some you can prepare yourself for and others hit you right in the face! We can become repetitive and rigid when we are preoccupied or in a negative mindset. By responding this way, we undervalue some emotions and overvalue others.

Negativity and rigidity can make us less resilient and increase our safety-seeking behaviours. To get out of this mode and become more agile we must realise what is happening. Make small adjustments to your mindset regarding everything that is currently challenging you. Ask yourself: what is an alternative and what is the worst thing that can happen? By opening yourself up to alternative methods of problem-solving, you will become confident. If you cannot think outside the box you must ask for advice, support or feedback from others.

Agility is considered a critical skill by employers. Research says that jobseekers should include in their resumes one or two instances in which they demonstrated agility. When have you introduced an initiative or adapted your working style?

ALCOHOLISM

Over time, excessive alcohol use can lead to the development of chronic diseases and serious problems including high blood pressure, heart disease, stroke, liver disease and poor digestion.

When our family lived in Darwin, we would often go to a popular local swimming hole. My parents would sit by the water drinking continuously and my siblings and I would swim and play all day long. Driving home was a nightmare. One day my father was drunk as usual, and his eyes were bright red and irritated from swimming and his excessive indulgence. He miscalculated a T-intersection and swung the car abruptly. My brother and two sisters were flung out while I somehow held onto a door handle. One sister was severely injured and required immediate hospitalisation. The others miraculously came away with only minor scratches and bruises.

I learnt that swimming and alcohol were not a good combination, and that I never wanted to get into a car with a drunk driver again.

This experience significantly affected me during my teenage years and later as a leader. Marriages and relationships are destroyed by alcohol abuse, and I saw this quite often during my years in schools. On several occasions I had to sit next to colleagues and monitor their drinking or speak to them about their behaviour at a function. When I was not around, their behaviour deteriorated. Alcohol abuse made complete fools of them and reflected badly on me as their leader. Do not disgrace yourself in the company of your colleagues or boss! Bosses are like elephants: we do not forget!

If you are drinking every day and it is affecting your relationships and productivity at work, you need to seek support as soon as possible. For women, it is excessive to have more than three drinks a day or seven a week. For men, it is four or more a day or 14 a week. If you drink more than the daily or weekly limit, you are at risk. What are the signs that someone has a problem with alcohol? They may show a lack of interest in previously normal activities and appear tired, depressed or irritable. They may seem to get intoxicated more regularly, are unable to say no to alcohol or drink more to achieve the same effects. Staff who rely heavily on drinking every day and take recreational drugs are not aware of how they appear at their workplace. I sent home a staff member who turned up to school drunk and another member of staff who was high on drugs.

I remember getting caught out at a romantic weekend away with my husband. I had the little black dress on and may have indulged in a few too many wines when we bumped into a family of six from my school while staying at the Crown Casino. I nearly died! I remember the look of amazement on the faces of the parents and four children. 'Hello, Mrs Patterson,' they said in unison. I flicked my hair out of my eyes, straightened myself up, put the puppies back in, removed my husband's hand from the back of my bottom and sheepishly said hello and walked out of the lift. You can guess what lesson I learnt that day!

ALIGNMENT MODEL

It took me many years as a leader to put everything together into a simple alignment equation. To make sense of all the variables in education, an arrangement in a straight line makes things easier to navigate. Bringing elements into alignment allows for proper coordination. My father took apart an old Holden bit by bit in Darwin, and I remember he put everything in a line on the front lawn. I watched him over the following weeks methodically realigning the parts from most important to least important. He cleaned and repaired some of the parts and, after what seemed like a lifetime, rebuilt the whole car. The end product was better and ran faster. I applied this thinking to my own leadership.

If the wheels of a school or organisation are out of alignment, then go back to the beginning and start again. You can apply this lineal structure to your narrative as a leader, educator or teacher.

Alignment model for educators

1. What is your moral purpose? I believe that in education we are morally obliged to work as hard as we can to get the desired results for our students. We should know what is right and wrong for them.
2. What are your students' learning needs? What other information applies to their year level?
3. Which programs best meet these needs? What are the demographics of the school?
4. When do you implement these programs?
5. Which Department of Education principles of practice do they align with?
6. Which teaching models do you use?
7. How do you teach?
8. How do you track impact, traction and progress?
9. Which quality-improvement tools do you use to plan, implement and evaluate progress?
10. What professional development or learning do you need to upskill yourself or your staff?
11. What would be the desired outcomes?
12. How will all of this build a better future for all?

ARROGANCE

Arrogant people are habitually reluctant to consider the possibility that they are wrong. I dealt with many of these types throughout my 46 years in education. All too often everyone else has to walk on eggshells around them.

People who are confident are certain about their ability and have faith in themselves. Confidence is very appealing; arrogance is usually fake confidence from someone trying to compensate for their insecurities by presenting themselves as superior to others.

Tips for dealing with arrogance

1. Make sure that your own confidence is high when speaking to them—if not, delay that conversation
2. Read Stephen Covey's *7 Habits of Highly Effective People*
3. Use the GROW mental model (Goal: what do you want? Reality: where are you now? Options: what could you do? Will: what will you do?)
4. Practice your tolerance and diplomacy skills
5. Do not call the person out unless you must, or you will invite an argument and further drama
6. Limit the information you divulge; hold some cards close to your chest for another time
7. If the meeting or conversation is not going in the right direction, defuse or distract with another topic
8. Shut the issue down and move on, or park it for now and revisit later

Timing is everything: is it worth the cost to your own health and wellbeing? If confrontation will add to your distress, avoid it. It is not the right time. Self-care is more important for you.

ATTITUDE

When I interviewed candidates for a position, I looked at resumes that addressed the selection criteria and listed the candidate's qualifications and experiences. I would ask questions related to the selection criteria and the interviewees would answer accordingly. But I was always looking for something different, something intangible. This was mindset and attitude.

A positive attitude is required for any workplace environment. A negative attitude should be avoided, especially when working with students, parents and in teams.

Individuals who believe their knowledge, skills and talents can be developed through demanding work, good strategies and input from others have a growth mindset. These are the type of teachers we want to be leading classrooms and instructing our students. These are the type of leaders we want leading and inspiring themselves and others.

BALANCE

When your workload increases along with mental, emotional and physical stress, you need to counterbalance the negative effects you'll be feeling. Doing something enjoyable after a demanding and difficult meeting, incident or time in your day neutralises the aftermath by exerting an opposite influence.

If I stayed after school for a meeting that went for several hours into my already long day, then I would go in later the next day or leave early the next day to counterbalance my long hours. I would make good use of this time by going for an early-morning walk or to the gym. My phone would always be on because technically I was on call for those hours, but I prioritised myself. It's key to get that balance and momentum in your life so you are always moving forwards and not going backwards. As a new principal, you must take slow and calculated steps. Although you may sometimes think you're not making a difference, being new means doing things for the first time: establishing systems within your school, updating the technical support, building relationships. It all takes time. Becoming a new leader or changing schools is a learning curve in your life, so give yourself permission to deal with the rocks firstly and let all the pebbles and sand go by the wayside for the moment. Say no more often and delegate more often. Stand on the balcony and lead from above, only coming down to the dance floor if necessary. Keep your head above water and more importantly be kind to yourself.

BEST VERSION OF YOURSELF

Our role as educators is to provide hope for students and others within our work environment and school communities. Being your best self inspires others. It is paramount to motivate and encourage others with a personal purpose and vision. Emitting a positive attitude and growth mindset in challenging times is helpful. Being in tune with your values, rising to the top and not engaging in negative or destructive thoughts are the keys to success.

How can you be the best version of yourself? Look at yourself in the mirror and like what you see: you are unique. If you do not like what you see, change your hair style or wardrobe. Second-hand shops are great! Put a bit of colour into your surroundings. Declutter your life, home and relationships. Get rid of any deadbeat partners and energy zappers in your life. Get outdoors and exercise and enjoy nature. And smile more! It costs nothing and lifts the mood. If you are not the best version of yourself and you know it, find support. Those we work and live with deserve nothing less. Seek medical advice, ask a friend or colleague for help and take the necessary steps towards feeling happier and healthier.

BODY LANGUAGE

Body language refers to facial expressions, posture, gestures, eye movement, touch and the use of space. Voice is also important, as is paying particular attention to inconsistencies. At school I often needed to read body language. I could tell when a student was lying to me simply by the way their face went red and by reading their gestures and erratic eye movements. I also used my observations when interviewing prospective staff and dealing with difficult parents. Watching verbal and nonverbal forms of communication helped me understand human nature. Nonverbal communication can be deliberate or unintentional, and cues are culture-bound. Nonverbal messages are often more trustworthy than verbal messages when the two conflict.

Some of the parents I dealt with were territorial in their behaviour, guarding and defending their children at all costs. Showing empathy and siding with them allowed me to convince them that we both wanted what was best for their children. Territorial behaviour was important to some parents because it gave them the impression of guarding their family and sense of identity. They would lose face if they did not defend their children in front of others. Sometimes it is a cultural trait. You must relate to and engage with someone before you can introduce any form of resolution. Understanding body language and verbal communication techniques helped me in many demanding situations. Understanding cultural behaviour also helped.

BOSSES

I find that bosses tend to come in five leadership types: participative, outspoken, experienced, bold and 'best friend'. You will find that one person can embody each type at different times depending on their personality. Some situations may call for more experience, some for daring ideas and others for collaboration. A good boss will adapt and delegate accordingly.

Three management styles

1. *I am the No. 1 boss*
   This style manages through clear direction and control. It is sometimes referred to as the autocratic or directive management style. Authoritarian managers typically assert strong authority, have total decision-making power and expect unquestioning obedience

2. *Ok, I'll include others*
   The democratic management style involves managers reaching decisions with the input of their employees but being responsible for making the final decision. Some other words that could be used to describe this style are consultative, participative and collaborative.
3. *Let's work together*
   These leaders have an attitude of trust and reliance on their employees. They do not micromanage, get too involved, or give excess instruction or guidance. They prefer to let their staff use their creativity, resources and experience to help them meet their goals.

I loved being a boss, but I knew that I was not everybody's cup of tea. While I often reflected upon my own actions, I noticed that some people who were inclined to comment on or judge my leadership style needed to look inward first! It is apparent when a lack of confidence and self-worth is contributing to feelings of intimidation. These people needed to feel less uncertain about themselves rather than projecting it onto me. I would like to be described as a woman who got the job done in a fair, orderly and efficient manner. Bosses cannot please everyone all the time. We are damned if we do and damned if we don't.

With this mindset, I stopped worrying about what others thought of me and remained focused on the goals and targets of the school. I did not expect staff to like me, but I did expect them to respect the status of the principal. Trust needs to be earned, and this is extremely hard when stepping into a new position. The brains of other people within the school or organisation need time to adjust to the new person: their voice, their image and their direction. Patterns within the brain develop continuously over a period, and so do people's opinions of you as a leader. Be kind to yourself and allow others the time to become familiar with you as their new leader during the process.

A great boss is honest and trustworthy, with the ability to inspire, motivate and mentor staff. They combine high emotional intelligence with open and honest feedback. They have a powerful sense of self-awareness and purpose. And, of course, they have the knowledge and skillset to perform the job.

Tips for dealing with bosses

1. Respect their position: for whatever reason, they are there in the top seat
2. Give them time to get used to the position and develop your trust
3. Be respectful: you never know when you will need their reference for another position
4. Recognise their personality traits and leadership style, and adapt when necessary
5. If they are a toxic person, limit your contact with them
6. If a toxic boss does anything inappropriate to you, see your line manager immediately
7. Watch and learn from them. If they are a good role model, what are they doing that inspires others? What is their leadership style and how do they adapt to different challenges? How do they contribute to a harmonious work culture?
8. Ask if they can coach or mentor you
9. Seek constructive feedback and be willing to learn
10. Acknowledge their birthday

Tips for future bosses

1. Learn on the job
2. Enjoy what you are doing and know your purpose
3. Know the goals and obstacles of your organisation
4. Dress, walk and talk like a boss
5. Tell your staff they matter and don't whine about them
6. Lead by example
7. Forgive when mistakes are made
8. Change is inevitable and life is not fair
9. Stop, look people in the eye and acknowledge them
10. Network and open opportunities for others
11. Support, recognise and reward your staff
12. Accept that not everyone will like you
13. Make your own judgements
14. Do not play it too safe

15. The worst thing you can do is nothing
16. Listen to your instinct
17. Family matters more than friends

BUDGETING

I first learnt that our family was poor one day when there was a knock at our door. We were living in Seven Hills, an outer suburb of Sydney. I was around three and my brother was four. My mother told us to hide under the kitchen table and be quiet. Ssshhh, she said, with her finger held up to her lips. She stood behind the kitchen door, hiding from the person who was knocking. I did not realise it at that moment, but it was the property owner coming for his rent. My parents were late again with their weekly rental payments.

I learnt that we lived day by day and that money was scarce. My parents never saved, and we lived on the smell of an oily rag.

Being fiscally capable and trained to understand budget-management reports, spreadsheets and statements is something that leaders need to master. Unfortunately, fiscal management is not taught in schools. If you don't know how you manage your own personal income, how are you expected to understand and manage a work budget? This is a recipe for disaster, in many cases involving fraud and fiscal mismanagement. I did not study accounting or finance at school, and was very much self-taught. I would listen to my mentors' stories of success and good financial management, as well as cautionary tales of fraud and bankruptcy.

Start by understanding what comes in as income and what goes out as expenditure. Understand the art of invoicing and keeping a paper trail for all financial interactions. Read the fine print and understand what you are signing. Take documentation home to read and unpack and seek further explanation if you still do not understand. Ask the dumb questions, because you will look more of a fool if a dodgy document is thrown in your face and the person on the other side of your desk reminds you that you signed it!

Lastly, do as many professional development training courses as you can. Ask a mentor or someone you really respect to meet with you to go over what you are planning. There are many support mechanisms in education, and so take up the offers of help from professional associations.

BULLYING

I wish I had a dollar for every time I heard this word thrown around incorrectly. School bullying, like bullying outside the school context, refers to one or more perpetrators who have greater physical or social power than their victim and act aggressively toward their victim by verbal or physical means. Bullying is when people repeatedly and intentionally use words or actions against someone or a group of people. In schools we must remember the difference between normal human development, rudeness or meanness and true bullying.

Mean is when a student is unkind or deliberately inconsiderate: 'You're ugly!'

Rude is when a student is disrespectful, impolite, inconsiderate or thoughtless: 'You stink!'

Bullying often takes the form of ongoing meanness or rudeness.

Tips for dealing with bullying or a lack of kindness

1. Use non-committal body language before any investigation begins
2. Show empathy
3. Assess and respond to the situation, not the person
4. Understand the context and use good questioning and listening techniques
5. Listen to all sides and address behaviours
6. Call on the student to identify their inappropriate behaviour

7. Let the victim express how the behaviour made them feel
8. Do not give too much time and attention to the student being rude, mean or a bully
9. Decide on boundaries and consequences
10. Document everything

CALM IN A CRISIS... HE HAS A GUN!

It was before school, and I was in my classroom preparing for the teaching day. An announcement came over the PA system calling me to the office. When I arrived, a teacher ran in and said that there was a father in the school yard armed with a gun looking for his son's teacher! She told us the student's name and my face went white. The student was in my class. I felt as if the roof was going to drop in. Suddenly in ran the father. 'Where is he?' he shouted. While I was confusedly wondering if he was talking about me, it suddenly became clear that he was after the art teacher. The boss and I managed to calm him down and found that his gun was a toy. A bloody toy!

Many years later I was at a wedding and recognised the eyes of the photographer. I had seen those eyes before. It was the student, and his father was assisting him with his photographic equipment. I just stared at them.

A similar incident played out again years later when an anonymous caller to my school alluded to the fact that a hitman was going to come onto school grounds to find a boy whose father had conned a man out of a large amount of money. We immediately made an announcement for all the students and teachers to remain in their classrooms because a swarm of bees had come onto our grounds, saying that we would let them know when they could leave after the bees had gone. This ploy bought us some time to ring Emergency Management and the police. I rang the boy's mother, and she came quickly and took her son off the grounds and safely home.

Yet another notable crisis started with a phone call. *Ring! Ring!* Mrs Patterson speaking, I answered. A voice at the other end urgently told me that I was needed in the Year 4 Gallery. There was a student threatening to kill and he wanted me! I dropped everything, ran up the yard and into the classroom, where I saw a boy by the window waving around a pair of scissors. I immediately told the Education Support worker to step aside and the teacher to remove all the other students from the classroom. As the boy furiously waved the scissors and verbally abused me, I noticed that it was the end of the school day. Parents would be outside and there was a crowd gathering. I raised my hand and said to him, 'Look, it's home time and I need a coffee. You like Milo, so how about we go down to the staff lounge and get a coffee for me, Milo with two sugars for you and a couple of chocolate biscuits, and have a chat?' He followed like a lamb.

I learnt several lessons from that incident: how to defuse challenging situations with humour, a level head and food; how to master the art of scissor-snatching and disarm a student holding a dangerous weapon; and to always have Milo, biscuits and other snacks on hand to calm volatile children.

Tips for defusing a difficult situation

1. Have a school-wide action plan so that everyone knows their part to play in any demanding situation
2. Have visual scripts on hand and displayed with easy access
3. Remove dangerous objects, get students out of the classroom and have an exit plan for yourself

4. Get behind a door, wall or car to avoid putting yourself on the frontline of danger
5. Contain anyone who is threatening others
6. Learn some self-defence techniques
7. Ring the police: set your phone communication up in a code alert system so you just have to press one button that sends a message to the police or another member of staff
8. Reassure the instigator that you are there to support them
9. Use open hands when speaking, and make gestures to say *stop, come here, lower the weapon, it's okay* or *you are all right*
10. Do not clench your fists; demonstrate calming body movements.
11. Contain the situation by lowering your voice and talking 'with instead of at' while you wait for backup
12. Use your empathic listening skills
13. If the person is holding a weapon, tell them in an assertive voice to put it down and repeat the statement if necessary
14. Remember the quote 'calm in a crisis'
15. Your job is to defuse, contain and get a positive outcome from the situation
16. Seek help if the situation is beyond your ability
17. Afterwards, arrange a debrief session with all involved and organise counselling or contact your employment assistance program for professional help if needed

Even if you don't find yourself faced with a scissors-wielding Grade 4 boy, you will experience crises in which you need to remain calm. How can you prepare for these events? I recommend learning the art of mediation. It will develop clear thinking and guide you through panic. If you are not ready to meet with a difficult person, then don't. Arrange via a phone call for a time and place to meet and always have someone with you. Always have a clear exit from your office or classroom. If the situation is out of your control, seek professional advice and support.

COACHING

Coaching is often confused with mentoring, and it is important to be aware of the similarities and differences between these significant tools that leaders use to improve performance.

Coaching more immediately relates to specific organisational requirements. Mentoring is done by someone with a relevant set of skills and experience. Mentors are mostly interested in the person and the content of the conversations, whereas coaches will additionally focus on the process of learning. Head to 'Mentoring' for more information.

The purpose of coaching is to help staff use their day-to-day work as a learning experience to recognise and take advantage of opportunities to improve their performance, knowledge and skills. The use of specific tasks is accompanied by ongoing performance appraisal and review.

Major features of a coaching approach to staff development

1. An ongoing process
2. Planned allocation of tasks or responsibilities
3. Regular appraisal of performance through formal feedback, discussion and review
4. The recognition that every task can have development potential

Good coaching techniques require a leadership commitment to the continuous development of staff training. Each task is a learning encounter. This approach has the benefit of allowing staff to realise that it is possible to work, learn and develop at the same time.

A coach focuses on the process of coaching conversations, in addition to looking at the person and their situation. The person being coached is encouraged to be responsible for their own learning. The coach will indirectly be accountable: how skilled are they at facilitating change?

Staff benefit from immediate feedback on their performance; their job satisfaction improves as their skills and work involvement increase. Their importance to the school becomes more apparent and they can see their leader not just as a manager, but as someone who genuinely cares for their professional development and is there to help.

The leader benefits from a more rewarding and productive team. They develop greater confidence in their staff, with whom they have strong and mutually beneficial working relationships. There are more opportunities for delegation, and the leader's own confidence and reputation grow as they become known as someone who inspires and develops their team's skills.

Typical school opportunities for coaching

1. Research-based action projects
2. School-based goals
3. An area of development that requires improvement
4. An unexpected situation with a fellow staff member or parent
5. A new area of responsibility
6. Professional development or upskilling
7. Classroom management

Skills needed to be an effective coach

1. Identifying training and learning needs
2. Observing and assessing
3. Questioning and listening
4. Explaining and demonstrating
5. Setting goals and expectations
6. Providing feedback

Questions for an effective coaching technique

1. What is on your mind today?
2. So, what is your real challenge?
3. And what else?
4. And what else? (Repeat this question twice or three times and remain quiet as they reply)
5. So, what is your real challenge?

When I used this coaching technique, I noticed that answers to the second question were very different to those given in response to the fifth question. People who are coached in this way will unpack their challenges and add further information to the issue they initially identify. If you accept their answer to the second question, you will not find out the whole story. Head to 'Ladders' to assist with your response as a coach.

CONFIDENCE

Schools require outgoing, confident people who are comfortable dealing with large groups and gatherings. How can you display confidence? You must show certainty about the things you believe in. Keep track of your achievements; if you believe that you have not achieved enough, it shows. Set goals to achieve outcomes. Think of the things you are good at. Everyone has their strengths, talents and skills; speak about yours in a confident manner. Always speak highly of yourself and talk about the things you love. Have skills, hobbies or interests that add to your repertoire. You do not have to be loudmouthed and extroverted to be confident.

Supremely confident people are often quiet and unassuming. They already know what they think: they want to know what the other person thinks. Confident people know that they know a lot, but often they want to know more, and they know the only way to learn more is to listen to others and learn from their stories. Working with and employing confident people is so rewarding. People who believe in their own abilities, skills and knowledge make others feel confident as well. The self-belief, self-reliance and self-awareness in confident people fosters greater relationships and successful outcomes.

Standing upright with correct posture is a real indicator of confidence. Correct posture puts the least amount of strain on your muscles and joints. Rounded, slouched shoulders are not a good look. Good posture leads to better breathing, back relief, improved mood, optimal digestion, reduced headaches and great function as you age. Not only that, but you look better! The posture of a prospective teacher conveys a wealth of information about their personality characteristics and how they are feeling. Sitting up straight indicates that a person is focused and paying attention.

Tips for showing confidence

1. Stand upright and tall
2. Look directly into people's eyes
3. Speak clearly at your natural pitch
4. Do not giggle or laugh after you speak
5. Do not smile nervously
6. Smile confidently when the time is right
7. Do not hold back or have awkward breaks in speech
8. Do not move around and fidget
9. If you are sitting in a chair, do not swing around
10. If you are standing, stand still and focused

If you are lack confidence, foster a positive mindset. Say to yourself: this may make me feel nervous, but I am up to the challenge, and I will be confident.

CURIOSITY

When a child's curiosity is aroused, it is inherently rewarding and pleasurable. Researchers have determined that dopamine, the brain's reward chemical, is linked to its curiosity state. Curious students are interested in exploring ideas, activities and experiences. Like curious teachers, they want to learn strategies to increase their scholarly and personal knowledge. Curiosity is key to learning.

When students are curious about a particular topic, they are much more likely to learn quickly and retain information. Children in their first year of formal schooling are curious about what they see and the connections they make in their own lives. They wonder about what they learn at school and at home, about nature and their family and friends. They are curious about their own growing bodies. I do not know how many times I had to talk to young children about what they should be showing others in the playground and what is meant to be kept private!

When teachers plan experiences for their students, curiosity should be at the forefront of their thinking. When students are curious, they are much more likely to stay engaged. In many classrooms you can identify the curious students because they have a desire to understand. They can be seen asking questions, reading books and going out of their way to learn more about their surroundings and the world.

If we use our curiosity strategically, it can improve the way we work. It allows us to see creative solutions that may be missed by others, to make wise decisions, and to increase our influence and impact. You can promote curiosity by keeping an open mind and not taking things for granted. Curious thinkers constantly ask questions, consider learning fun and thrive on reading diverse kinds of literature.

Curiosity cannot be taught but can be illuminated and nurtured in the right learning environment. The same advice applies to leaders: if you create the right work culture, then staff thrive. Leaders who create positive learning environments are crucial to our education system.

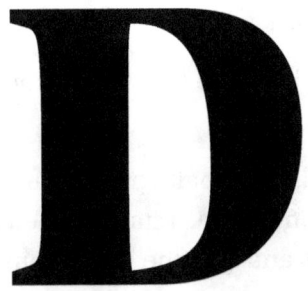

DECLUTTERING

Decluttering is a way of cleansing, refocusing and resetting yourself. A good clean-out every year gives you a fresh start. Spring is the best time to declutter. Throw away the stuff you have not used within the last three years. If you are braver, throw out everything you have not used in the last 12 months. Documents for the Education Department are kept for seven years, so don't throw those out! I learnt early on that you also need to declutter your relationships. When I had breast cancer, I remember my oncologist telling me not to be around negative, energy-sapping people. I tried as often as I could to surround myself with positive, energetic, grateful and supportive people. If I sat next to a negative person, I would often get up and walk away without worrying about the quality of my excuse. On some occasions I would not even explain why I had left, because I would not waste my time or engage in negative discussions. It was a habit that became second nature to me.

DEPARTMENT OF EDUCATION

Having success with important decisions is a real art. All decisions in life involve some risk-taking. Some people play it safe, but to be a successful leader you must be willing to take risky action in the hope of a desired outcome. Do your homework first. I used the ladder of inference method to assist with risk (see 'Ladders').

Every risky situation or challenge has an unavoidable loss: something is given up to achieve growth.

During my later years as a principal, I tried as much as possible to change legislation in our education system. It started when I won a high-performing principal award in 2010 and got the opportunity to travel to England and Ireland to research early-years readiness programs. I could see that educators in Australia needed to rethink the way we prepared children for their first year of school. Upon my return to Australia, I introduced an early-years readiness program called '2YPP' at Mill Park Heights Primary School. I did this with the permission of the Minister of Education at the time.

My primary concern was to identify students who would need two years of Prep instead of one. We found that 30 children out of the 160 enrolled were not ready for their first year of formal education. With the support of their parents, we piloted two classes of 15 students led by teachers who had taught in England and were familiar with the program. We trialled this venture for six years with amazing success, as confirmed by researchers from RMIT Bundoora who tracked the students over a six-year period.

However, it appeared that the program contravened government legislation. I received a letter from the Department of Education ordering me to discontinue our efforts. I was worried that I would be accused of misappropriation of funds, so I pulled the program. The parents supported the program and the students gained enormously, but there was nothing to be done.

We saw unbelievable changes in those students who had an extra year to develop their social and emotional skills. They were more resilient, had better decision-making skills and enjoyed better outcomes. Even when you know something is beneficial, your risky decision can be knocked on its head. Although disappointing, the end of the two-year Prep program did not stop me from being a risk-taker. If I had to do it all over again, I would.

DO IT EVERY DAY

Daily routines increase efficiency, reduce anxieties and leave us with more time for the things that we enjoy.

An easy routine to take you from morning to night

1. Prepare your clothing the night before, choosing colours and fabrics that makes you feel good
2. Organise your day, including when you will exercise and what you will eat
3. Visualise your activities
4. Remember your purpose of the day and take your time
5. Shower to feel clean, refreshed and well-groomed
6. Have a heathy breakfast and organise lunch and tea
7. Eat slowly and drink lots of water
8. Check your diary and to-do list
9. Keep visualising the day and cross out completed tasks. If tasks are important or urgent, do them today. If they can wait, do not prioritise them. Delegate tasks to others or save some for tomorrow.
10. Remember your phone, laptop, chargers, notes, stationery, grooming products (brush, mouth spray, lipstick, face mist, hair spray, tissues) and anything else you need
11. Greet people with a smile, say hello in a cheerful manner and enjoy the act of socialising
12. Avoid drama and negative people
13. Be present in meetings and when talking to people
14. Regularly get up from your desk and walk around to get some fresh air and sunlight during the day
15. Aim for 10,000 steps per day

16. Turn off technology after 6pm so your body can wind down. Prepare for sleep, soften the lighting and read
17. Take a warm shower, prepare your clothing for the next day and get your 8–9 hours of sleep

DO NOT CROSS THE LINE

This is an extremely sensitive topic at any workplace, but it is a conversation that I have had with staff over the years. Extramarital affairs or illicit hook-ups between teachers or parents are common occurrences at school. These types of relationships can cause enormous damage to work culture, staff morale and families. Inappropriate behaviour ignored becomes the norm. As a leader I was sometimes called upon to meet with the parties concerned to have exceedingly difficult conversations.

On one occasion, a parent rang me at school to allege that one of my staff was having an affair with his wife. I was in shock. My hands were shaking, and I almost lost it. I listened intently and knew that he was right, but had to remind him that he risked an accusation of character defamation. He left the situation with me and agreed to not do anything, and I got back to him after I had investigated his allegations. Unfortunately, he was right. I sought legal advice and dealt with the situation respecting the anonymity of all parties concerned.

As teachers and leaders, we cannot cross any lines with parents, colleagues or students. We need to keep our personal and professional lives separate. Uncomfortable though they were, these situations taught me a lot about holding people accountable and sometimes terminating their employment when necessary.

Be aware that people have different interpretations of competent work relationships. An official interpretation of appropriate relationships needs to be made clear. Leaders should be aware of staff interactions at work and particularly at after-work functions. If someone crosses the line with another staff member, they need to be held accountable. If the behaviour is of a sexual nature and can be considered harassment, encourage the victim to go to the police and make a report. Always bring inappropriate behaviour to the attention of someone in your organisation, preferably your line manager or boss. Seek professional advice from your organisation's legal team or the Department of Education conduct and ethics branch. Be brave and not do avoid or ignore the situation.

Keep documentation of your involvement with challenging people and situations. If you must record a conversation, let those involved know. I recorded many unsavoury telephone conversations as evidence. Never try to conceal or be dishonest because it will always come back to bite you when you least expect it. As I found out many times, what you think you said is not always what the other person thinks you said.

Protocols for meetings about inappropriate behaviour

1. Do any background checks beforehand
2. Outline the protocols of the meeting or conversation
3. Agree on the process
4. Use the GROW mental model as a guide (see 'Arrogance' for a reminder)
5. Agree that it is fine if any party wants to finish, leave or reschedule the meeting
6. Agree to respect each other's opinions, to listen, to record and to find a solution
7. Agree to disagree and to have different opinions, but do so in a respectful manner
8. Keep in mind your goal of finding a mutually optimal solution
9. Have an exit plan in case the meeting does not go well
10. Control and lead the meeting, unless it is the first occurrence and the person just wants to vent. In that case, listen. Use the WAIT strategy: 'why am I talking?'
11. Learn mediation techniques
12. Have the furniture in your office set up so that you are in the dominant position

13. Be conscious of your clothing: suit attire means formal, while soft pastels mean nurturing and compassionate
14. Know when a meeting or conversation is not going well, and call in the agreed protocols to let the other person know of your intention to reschedule

Never accept screaming, swearing or violence. Put your hand up and say stop. Indicate that the conversation will have to finish due to the person's disrespect and ask them to leave the room. If they do not leave, walk out. Always protect your safety. Never take your eyes off the aggressor and never turn your back on them. Be courteous, calm and in control when you ask them to leave. Warn others outside and walk the difficult person offsite. You may need to call the police or security.

You could follow up with a letter outlining their inappropriate behaviour and indicating that they would have to adhere to the positive behaviour guidelines if another meeting were to be scheduled. If the behaviour repeats itself, you could refer to your state or territory's trespassing laws.

EATING WELL

In a 2014 study published in the *British Journal of Health Psychology*, adults who consumed a healthy diet over 13 days experienced an increase in wellbeing and felt that their work gave them greater meaning and purpose. Healthy eating, active living and a positive outlook reduce risk of heart disease and some forms of cancer. Food has a direct impact on our cognitive performance, which is why poor decisions at lunch can derail an entire afternoon. Everything we eat is converted by our bodies into glucose, which provides the energy that our brains need to stay alert. Lunch is an opportunity to help our bodies.

Eating at your desk is a definite no. You need to get up and out of your office. Your desk is 400 times dirtier than your toilet, says Charles Gerba, a professor of environmental microbiology at the University of Arizona. Always wash your hands before and after eating, choose a clean table and use a napkin. Take your time and chew every bite.

ENERGY AND STAMINA

Stamina is the ability to sustain prolonged physical or mental effort. It is not about being the fastest to complete something; stamina beats speed.

I like to use the analogy of the tortoise and the hare when leading a project or starting something new. To complete a project on time or on budget, we must first make sure we have the stamina to do it right and see it through to the end.

Colleagues, students and parents often commented on my abundant amount of energy. I would bounce out of bed every day and race to work. It was not that I had so much work to complete, but that I absolutely loved my job. The thought of seeing the faces of my students every day, saying hello to the parents, chatting with my staff and being in a school environment brought me enormous joy.

As the saying goes, the meaning of life is to find your gift and the purpose of life is to give it away.

Teaching was my gift. Leading a school was also my gift. When you know your purpose in life, it shows: your demeanour radiates through your daily actions. It also shows in your energy levels. Teaching long hours without tiring requires a high level of stamina.

How can you increase your stamina? Prioritise physical health by exercising daily, eating well and drinking lots of water. For relaxation, try meditation or yoga. Music also relaxes your body and is nice to have on in the background in your office, classroom and home. Get outdoors and be with nature. Breathe in the air and the perfumes of the plants, listen to the sounds of the birds and get lots of sunshine. Elevated stamina allows you to perform your daily activities at a higher level while using less energy. Teaching can be incredibly stressful, so stamina is important. Low mood, depression and low self-confidence can cause poor stamina. Good stamina leads to better resilience and less fatigue, hardship and illness.

ENTHUSIASM

As a principal, I wanted enthusiastic teachers to teach and be role models for our students. Enthusiastic teachers feel good about themselves and are great to be around. They show interest in their students and what they do. Enthusiasm translates into passion. There are few things more enjoyable than talking enthusiastically about something you are passionate about, and feeling others share your enthusiasm. Teachers with enthusiasm are infectious and inspiring. Students with enthusiastic teachers complete their tasks with better focus. Happy students enjoying their learning it is a ticket for success. When teachers are enthusiastic and passionate, staff morale goes up and the organisational culture of the school or workplace is improved. The school's goals, targets and desired outcomes will be achieved at a quicker rate.

EYES ON THE PRIZE

Knowing your purpose, whether it be in life or whatever you are planning, enables you to look to the future. Goals and targets give your life meaning. They can focus on the short, medium or long term. When I had my stroke, I knew that my goals in life needed to change. I really did not have an alternative: if I continued what I was doing, I would more than likely have another stroke. I had to reassess my purpose in life, especially because I wanted to live a long time. First, I allowed myself to get better. I attended numerous doctor's appointments, blood tests and speech lessons. Second, I allowed myself to process what had happened and give my body time to recover. I gave myself permission to cry. I cried for six months before I could regain control of my life. Then I set short-term goals. I was going to walk five kilometres every day. After six months I increased my walking to 10 kilometres per day. When I walked, I was in the moment. I listened to podcasts and music, taking time to breathe in the fresh air and immerse myself in nature. There is something about long walks in the bush that is very spiritual. My short-term goals became medium-term goals, and then I set long-term goals. Step by step, day by day, week by week, month by month. After 18 months I was back to being fitter, healthier and more in tune with my body, mind and spirit. I stopped full-time work, set up my own consulting business and trained to become a mentor. All the while I kept my eye on the future and never looked back!

FAIR, FIRM AND FUN

Firm, fair leadership encourages people to work to the best of their ability in an environment where they can expect regular feedback. The success of my leadership meant that I usually got the desired outcomes for which I had planned. I did my homework, having learnt early that avoiding it often led to disaster. Due diligence and background checks gave me confidence that I was on the right track, even if I had to put in more hours. It is better to work harder at the beginning of a project or appointment than to deal with the ramifications that come with fallout!

How to practice firm and fair leadership

1. Being clear with staff and students about rules and responsibilities
2. Aways letting others know of your expectations
3. Not assuming that others know what your expectations are: repeat them often

4. Being consistent in how you apply rules and consequences
5. Treating others as you want to be treated
6. Always following through
7. Not promising consequences that you cannot or will not follow through on
8. Having a repertoire of language that you can use instead of saying an outright no

Fun is THE most important word in education and in life. It has a direct effect on motivation levels, determining what we learn and how much we remember. Learning through fun experiences should be promoted in all schools. This comprehensive approach to education has the goal of nurturing passion and continuous development along life's journey. By driving motivation through engaging experiences, we can promote the wellbeing of students and educators.

When working with your students, be active and show them that you are having fun. Have a great 'hook' or introduction to a topic. The whole-part-whole method is a good way to structure your teaching: introduce the overall picture of a task or lesson, deconstruct all the components to be mastered, and finally piece everything together into a complete whole again. Breaking your lessons up into phases allows for an alternation between brain activity and brain rest.

Teach to the whole class and give students choices: they all have different learning styles just as teachers have different teaching styles. Learning through play and games is important. Make sure to use concrete materials and hands-on activities. Some popular games to engage children in academic learning are puzzles, Buzz, bingo, marbles, Pictionary, snakes and ladders, Monopoly, Cluedo, snap and Uno. Encourage curiosity and creativity by varying your learning experiences both in and out of the classroom. Get up, move around and explore nature.

When teachers use activities and experiences that make learning engaging and fun, students are more willing to participate and take risks. Make the classroom a safe place for learning. Having fun helps students retain information because the experience is enjoyable and memorable.

Being in the excitement zone increases brain activity. Effective teachers set goals, make lists, ask questions, empower students and show interest in their learning. A boring learning environment is detrimental to learning. An average teacher gets average results! Spending several years with average teachers diminishes a student's growth. Building teacher capacity to improve student engagement and growth is so important in our schools.

Good teachers know how to engage the seven types of learners in their classrooms: visual, auditory, verbal, logical/mathematical, physical/kinaesthetic, social/interpersonal and solitary/intrapersonal. Students depend on their senses to process the information around them. A good teacher uses all learning styles to enhance student learning. Several studies suggest that happiness can influence a student's academic progress and cognitive development. When interviewing a new teacher, I looked for the 'fun' element. Did they smile, have a sense of humour, laugh? Were they the type of teacher we needed to educate and inspire our students?

FOOLS

A fool is a person who acts unwisely or imprudently. It is not my intent in this section to be disrespectful when I use this word—I am also referring to myself on many occasions! But not all fools are silly or senseless. Many of those whom I encountered in education were repeat offenders who knew what they were doing and marched on full steam ahead with no consideration of the fallout.

Throughout my career as a leader, I dealt with many foolish staff members: those who got drunk at staff functions, those who said things they shouldn't have, those who deceived, stole or gossiped about others. We must maintain self-awareness, consideration of others and responsibility for our own behaviour—particularly when we work with children. Schools now comply with conflict-of-interest declarations, stringent auditing processes and anti-corruption commissions. Foolish behaviour will always be found out.

Gossip is sometimes seen as a way of bonding staff. I believe that as a rule of thumb we should not talk about others because it tends to get back to them. Staff love talking about the new principal, but the walls of the office have ears! If you cannot speak nicely about someone, do not say anything. Follow this rule and you will get further in your career and be seen as someone who has principles. Gossip less and there will be less drama in your life.

It was the underperforming staff who really frustrated me: those who were slack, not on time, not prepared for their students. Some partied all night, took recreational drugs and behaved inappropriately. This often meant that I had to begin the process to their cancel their contracts or even cease their employment. I can honestly say that these teachers are now in the minority. Most of the teachers I have met and worked with were passionate, gutsy, committed and dedicated to their profession. More importantly, they made a difference with the students they worked with, inspiring them to go on to be successful adults with good career opportunities.

FORESIGHT, OVERSIGHT AND INSIGHT

Foresight is the ability to predict what will happen or be needed in the future. Leaders with foresight can determine necessary and appropriate actions to take. Initial hard work pays off: detailed plans promote foresight. It is essential for a leader to have a Plan A, a Plan B and a Plan C. In schools it is important to set money aside for emergencies and unexpected expenses that arise.

Tips for building your foresight

1. Improve your knowledge: the more you know about your role or a subject, the easier it will be to find similarities with your other areas of expertise
2. Build your experience: the more often you experience a particular problem, the better you become at finding solutions
3. Think: consider what might or will happen to improve your line of thought

4. Make predictions: based on the information you have at hand and your prior experience, you can make small predictions that you can use to shape plans
5. Play devil's advocate (something I did a lot as a principal): taking this stance allows you to contrast the obvious, the worst and the best possible scenarios

In contrast, oversight is an unintentional failure to notice or do something. Oversights are usually the result of inattention or inexperience. All leaders make mistakes at some point in time. For instance, failing to add a staff member to your staffing profile could cost you many thousands of dollars. I did this and it put my school's global budget out $100,000. Luckily, I had put aside some funds for an emergency. But it was an oversight that I never repeated.

GOALS

If you don't have goals, you're like a boat without a rudder. Goals give you direction and boost your motivation and self-confidence. Career goals can be short-term, medium-term or long-term. At work, my goal was to be an inspiration to others, to become a thoughtful and caring leader and to learn how to lead a school effectively.

There are three types of goals: process, performance and outcome. Process goals are specific actions or processes of performing. Performance goals are based on personal standard. Outcome goals are based on winning. Achievable goals are the pinnacle of a smart goal-setting strategy. They keep you focused on the right path. I often used the following model to set achievable goals that aligned with my values.

SMART is an effective tool that provides the clarity, focus and motivation you need to achieve your goals. It can improve your ability to reach these goals by encouraging you to define your objectives and set a completion date.

SMART goalsetting

Specific: Write down your goal with as much detail as possible.

Measurable: Identify quantitative targets for tracking your progress and results.

Achievable: Make sure it is possible to achieve the desired result.

Realistic: Goals must be relevant and important to you and should help you achieve larger objectives.

Timeframe: Goals are to be locked into a specific timeframe. When do you need the goal to be achieved?

Setting goals that are too easy will not move people to achieve more than their minimum potential. They miss the opportunity for growth, and they will never know what they might have achieved had the goal been more challenging. In schools, not only do the staff lose out on achieving the desired outcomes but we also short-change our students. There were a few times in my career as a leader when I felt disillusioned with goal-setting choices. I wish I had spoken up more when I noticed this, instead of delegating and trusting others to do the job.

Tips for setting goals

1. Look at your current situation: what did you do in the past? Where are you now? What do you want to improve on and achieve?
2. Follow the SMART formula
3. Write your goals down and put them on display to stay strong and committed
4. Break down each goal into small, manageable steps so you don't get overwhelmed
5. Celebrate and reward yourself to reinforce the positive actions you have taken so you can continue along your path
6. Learn effective systems and habits that make it easier for you to accomplish your goals daily

GUTS, COURAGE, GRIT AND GRUNT

The word 'guts' is significant for me. Guts means personal courage and determination, toughness of character. Sometimes it means trusting your instinct. I remember one meeting when I smelled something fishy and needed to muster up my courage to have a very tricky conversation.

We were extending our gymnasium after receiving a federal grant. I had a meeting scheduled with the architect, the builder and school personnel. The architect had just been for a long lunch meeting and apologised for being late. As soon as our meeting began, I caught a strong whiff of red wine and garlic. This was a strange smell considering we were in a school office. We went for a walk around the new build, and I noticed a bow in the wall of the extension. I asked if it was normal for new builds to have such obvious bows in their walls. 'Do not worry your pretty little head—you look beautiful today, Deborah!' said the architect. Well, that was it. I cancelled the meeting immediately. I was furious. The architect was shocked and wanted to know why. I said that he reeked of wine, had eaten too much garlic and was slurring his words. No, I was not going to make the next progress payment until the wall was corrected! A couple of weeks later we found out that the builder had gone bankrupt. I put in a formal complaint to the Department of Education and to the Master Builders Association of Victoria. Funny thing, we never saw the architect or builder onsite again!

Having a family of tradespeople can come in handy at times. As a leader, you will deal with professionals such as builders whose expertise may intimidate you. However, you don't have to be a builder to notice when something isn't right. What is your gut telling you?

Tips for being in control during construction projects

- You don't have to be an architect, engineer, or tradesperson to have an educated opinion
- Ask lots of questions about any project management involving your workplace

- Use a project-scheduling tool such as a Gantt chart to monitor progress
- Know the work expectations, the timelines and especially the budget
- Agenda budget updates at every meeting and know the deadlines for progress payments
- Accept that you will not know everything, but ask for jargon to be explained in terminology that you understand
- Record everything
- If it does not look or feel right, then question, question, question!
- Seek advice from the authorities overseeing the project
- Do not make an unscheduled progress payment even if a contractor demands one: if the progress payment it is out of sequence, stick to the payment agreement
- Always allow 10–15% of contingency funds to be set aside for variations
- Record every variation and make sure you agree with it and put that in writing
- Keep a separate record of variations, as this will affect your remaining contingency funds
- Be extra careful if you are a woman
- If it smells like a rat, it is a rat! Trust your gut!

People with courage take risks. I became accustomed to taking risks as I grew in experience, but I would not recommend it to a new leader. When leaders are starting out, they need to play it safe and do the right thing by the Department of Education guidelines. Risk-taking requires preparedness: I always did my due diligence before starting a new project, going to the relevant forums or training courses and reading all the documentation. (Or almost all of it... If I'm honest, I did not always read every single word!)

If I was still unsure, I would ring one of my colleagues or seek advice from someone reputable. The more experienced I became as a leader, the bolder I was and the more risks I took. However, I definitely did not play around with government funding or numbers. I did not want to end up in a grievance process at the Merit Protection Board or an anti-corruption commission!

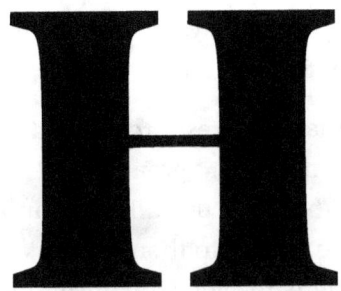

HAPPINESS

Happiness, like confidence, is an important quality in a leader. When I was recovering from my breast cancer, my oncologist told me to not surround myself with negativity. Negative people will bring you down and derail your progress, he said. When I returned to full-time work, I would deliberately get up and relocate myself to a more positive conversation or environment when the need arose.

There are four quadrants in which we find ourselves at various times. These are the happy, contented, conscientious quadrant; the survival-mode quadrant; the prisoner quadrant; and, most toxic of all, the whiner quadrant. We move in and out of these throughout life and in our work environments. When I took up my principalship in different schools, I would be in the survival quadrant. My aim would to be move after a brief period to the happy quadrant. People who are in the prisoner quadrant must often be convinced to move up to the happy quadrant. This often happens when you are introducing change and find that some people must be dragged along for the journey. Some people embrace change willingly and others only accept it begrudgingly.

Refusing to change can often be a sign of ignorance, obstinance or arrogance. People fear for their security, avoid anything different and want to protect themselves. As leaders, we must try to understand where these people are coming from and what they are fearing. Listen, engage in dialogue and make them feel valued.

As a leader, I strove to make the resources I had work for me. Make your staff work for you. If you moan and groan about your staff, you will be on a downhill slope. Build them up, upskill them and change their negative mindset to a positive one. Listen to them and take on some of their ideas but maintain accountability for your organisation. Do not sell your soul! Do not be extorted emotionally. If your intentions are genuine and your insight is on target, then others will have to get on board or get off. I used to say to my staff that they had three choices with change: buy in, block or bow out. The first option is the preferred one, the second option will involve further work and for the third option, I will hold the door open!

Tips for increasing your happiness

1. Include the word happiness in your purpose statements
2. Have the guts to move on when dealing with challenging issues
3. Do not waste time dwelling on problems
4. Know that change is inevitable, and welcome challenges: happy people believe that with change comes success
5. Remain positive
6. Be kind, assertive and unafraid to speak up when needed
7. Always have backup plans
8. Take risks, or you will remain idle
9. Acknowledge other people's happiness and enjoy being surrounded by likeminded people

HEAD, HEART AND HAND

Lead with your head, heart and hand. The head contains intelligence and knowledge. The heart contains love. The hand takes responsibility for demanding work. Leaders who lead with the head focus on big-picture goals and outcomes. Leaders who lead with the heart know how to engage, coach and motivate people. Leaders who lead with their hands know the tactical tools and skills needed.

Head, heart and hand leaders use their power *with* people, not over people. They have a vision that motivates others to perform beyond self-interest, seeking the greater good for their team. This concept of leadership translates into a model for action.

How to lead using your head, heart and hand

Head: What is the rational basis for change?

Heart: Do you have the emotional attachment and commitment to the change?

Hand: What are the actions that must be taken for change to occur?

HUMOUR AND LAUGHTER

I dealt with many difficult and interesting parents during my 22 years as a principal, from the father who reminded me that he had been in jail for murder to the one who said he wanted to rearrange my face. My reply to the convicted murderer was: 'Well, I had better be nice to you!' I asked permission of the second father to put my lipstick on before he rearranged my face. Humour was my way of defusing tricky and challenging moments. In fact, humour is my way of dealing with life in general. It's a method of keeping the peace that can make others feel content however unreasonable they may be.

Leaders who want to be role models should stay away from sarcasm. Whenever I saw leaders use sarcasm, it always harmed their relationships.

You cannot please everyone even when situations are diffused with humour. A person who pleases others and puts their own pleasure on the backburner will get hurt. Be sure, be purposeful and be in the moment. Understand the situation and read the play. Sometimes we must stay within our comfort zone to protect ourselves, and other times we must learn new adaptive skills.

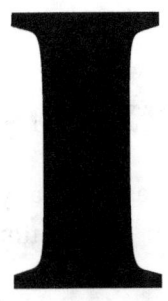

INTERVIEWS

How should you behave during an interview? Do you have to play the game or be yourself? I went for 26 interviews for positions as an advanced skilled teacher in the 1980s. I also went to 14 interviews for principal positions, so I consider myself a bit of an expert on this topic. I am outgoing, can be loud at times and like a good laugh. Can you imagine interviewing someone like me?

I could write a book on the bloopers and disasters of interviews that I experienced up the ladder of success. Where to start? Once I used the 'take a breath' technique to think through an answer and took so long that I forgot the question! Another time I wore an angora jumper that made me sweat; not only that, but I became sick from the fluff coming off the jumper and into my mouth. For another interview I decided to wear glasses to make me look older, but left them on the desk afterwards. A panel member told me that I had forgotten my glasses and I replied, 'Oh that's fine, they were only props to make me look older.' As you can imagine, these bloopers cost me the positions.

When you go for an interview, be sincere. It is imperative to show genuine interest in the school, position and the students. When I interviewed applicants, I looked for positivity, honesty and actual examples that were factual and reflective.

Interview skills to set you apart

1. Do your research to find out as much as you can about the organisation
2. Thoroughly review the job description and typical duties in that position
3. Prior planning prevents poor performance: re-read the job description and requirements before the interview
4. Arrive 30 minutes early to allow for traffic and delays, then sit in the car and check that you have everything
5. Tidy your hair and check your teeth and makeup (if you're wearing any). Freshen your breath and check that your buttons are done up and zip is closed. Women: make sure your boobs are tucked in and avoid see-through clothing. If you're unsure of the dress requirements, dress more formally. The more professional your actions, the more pleasant you appear to employers!

Clear communication is essential for any job interview. We communicate not only through our words, but also through our body language and appearance. Take pride in how you present yourself and any documents you share.

Interview communication tips

- Address the interview panel by their names
- Be prepared for small talk at the beginning of the interview, and have some courteous questions on hand
- Get your breathing regulated

- Keep your voice at a volume that is not too loud and not too low
- Avoid interrupting the person asking you questions
- Do not overuse jargon; explain the meaning of any abbreviations you use
- No 'ums': don't be afraid to think before you speak
- Watch how everyone is sitting, and mirror their body language
- Be aware of your own body language to ensure you are presenting yourself in a professional and positive way
- Listening skills are important: if you did not hear the question correctly ask, for it to be repeated
- Ask questions if you to gain a better understanding
- Arrive with a few questions about the job on hand
- Talk about your experience, accomplishments and abilities in a confident way that conveys your belief in yourself to perform the duties of the position
- Show interest and let them see that you are the right fit for the position
- As soon as the final decision has been made, seek feedback if you are not the successful applicant. There is a position out there for you, so don't give up!

Sample answers to interview questions

Always have a two-minute introduction about yourself. Start with what you are doing currently, then work your way backwards. Do not bore your interviewers with a long speech. Offer a couple of sentences that precisely describing you.

> *My four years' experience in a call centre and hospitality have taught me a great deal about dealing with customers. I have developed strong problem-solving skills, honed my ability to manage conflict and deal with demanding individuals, and polished my communication skills. I am keen to use my passion for excellent customer service to provide the best possible experience for your students to learn.*

Describe yourself in one word.

I would choose the word versatile. I can quickly adjust to different situations. In my previous job I successfully dealt with customers who had unique demands. I had to continually change my approach to meet their specific needs and get the desired results.

I would say results-driven. I have successfully achieved several personal goals this year including running a marathon, upgrading my computer skills and starting a new hobby. I set myself challenges and work hard to meet them.

Tell me something about yourself that is not in your resume.

I am a terrific dancer, a good cook, a long-distance runner and a Bombers fan. These interests will make me a well-rounded future teacher.

How have you responded to negative feedback?

I know that critical feedback is valuable, and it is important to react constructively. If the person is upset, I first acknowledge their emotion. Then I calmly ask factual questions to fully understand the feedback and gain clarity. This reduces the emotion and gives me the time and information I need to respond properly. If I discover I have made a mistake, I thank them for pointing it out and describe what I will do to fix it or prevent it happening again. If I am not sure the feedback is correct, then I tell them I appreciate their input but need some time to consider it and I will get back to them.

How do you handle an uncooperative colleague?

I address the uncooperative behaviour when it occurs. I plan the conversation as much as possible beforehand and choose a private place to calmly discuss the situation. My first objective is to determine the reasons for the lack of cooperation, so I start by factually describing the incident of uncooperative behaviour and the impact it had. I am careful to use 'I' statements to describe my concerns to avoid the conversation becoming accusatory.

> *I explore why the incident happened, focusing on the situation and not the person. I remain unemotional, listen closely to the explanation, display empathy and ask questions until I have sufficient information to determine a way forward. We discuss and agree on any changes that are needed and how and when they will be made.*

What is your main weakness and why?

> *I tend to take on too much because I have ambitious standards and get impatient when others do not meet them. But I am working on my delegating skills and learning how to let others do their jobs while I do mine.*

> *I do not yet have solid experience in....*

> *I am currently taking an online course in/teaching myself/ researching... and I look forward to making use of these skills as my teaching career develops.*

How did you handle a tricky situation?

> *I was able to deal with the situation by gathering and considering all the relevant facts to identify the underlying issues. I could then objectively determine different approaches to address these issues and decide on the most appropriate one.*

What motivates you? (Your answer should match up with the requirements of the position.)

> *Using my problem-solving skills and perseverance to overcome a challenge is personally satisfying. Successfully completing a task accurately and on time gives me a sense of accomplishment and motivates me to do an excellent job.*

Why should we hire you?

> *I have a strong work ethic. I am a fast learner, and I am very enthusiastic about this school and the position. I believe that my motivation and commitment will ensure that I quickly become a productive, supportive and valued member of your team.*

Where do you see yourself in five years? (It is advisable to answer in general terms when faced with this typical interview question.)

> *I want to have grown within my work, to have increased my responsibilities and skills. I enjoy a challenge and would like to know that I am constantly meeting new challenges. My goal is to be the best at whatever level I am working at with the school.*

How would you deal with a colleague who threw you under the bus for something that was their fault?

> *Office politics is always fun, right? I would start by taking it up with the person directly. I do not think there is anything to gain from publicly humiliating anyone, even if they just tried to do it to me. I would also make sure that my boss privately understood the reality of what went on: what my role was in the issue, whether I shared any of the blame, and what I did to help resolve the problem.*

Questions for the panel

Be careful with questions, because they could either go in your favour or dramatically backfire. I tend to play it safe. I thank the panel for their time, call them by their names, look them in the eye, shake hands and say that I look forward to receiving that phone call. The following questions are a good bet:

1. Why is the position being advertised?
2. Which area of the school/organisation will I be working in?
3. What are the main skills needed to master the job?
4. What is the most important part of the role?

5. What do you enjoy most about working here?
6. When are you looking to start the right candidate?
7. Can I have a quick tour?

You could finish with something like this:

> *I am certain that the skills I developed in my previous position, including my planning and organisational ability, my problem-solving skills and my experience working in a diverse team will readily transfer into success in this job. I am eager to combine my set of valuable competencies with my enthusiasm for this role to quickly become an asset to your school.*

JOURNEYS AND PATHWAYS

We cannot ever know what is coming, and need to enjoy each day instead of trying only to get to our destination.

Where are you going? Why are you doing along the path? Clarity, direction and purpose are important on our travels throughout life. Plan and give meaning to what you are doing and where you want to be in the future. Being too spontaneous is risky when you are responsible for others.

There were times in my career when I did not know what an outcome would be or if I could get to a solution that met all expectations. In those situations, I turned my negative mindset into a positive. I concluded that the issues I was dealing with were always going to be something that a principal had to face, so I needed to get with the program. I began to enjoy the unfolding process and worked with it instead of against it. It was hard at first, but it got easier year after year.

JUGGLING

We all have roles in life. I was a principal, wife, mother, daughter, daughter-in-law, sister, auntie, cousin, friend, volunteer, neighbour, mentor and coach. No one is a superwoman or superman. We cannot do all life's roles, but we can learn to move in and out of a particular role depending on the situation.

Staying organised helps you keep a clear head, so you can picture what you need to do and when. Set goals in your professional and personal lives. Prioritisation is key: what needs to come first? What role do I need to be in? What is important? What is urgent? What can be delegated? What can I let go of? Remember to listen to your body and develop wellbeing strategies. What are they and how often can you use them? Using a calendar not only enables you to keep track of appointments, but also allows you to deliberately block sessions into your day for exercise, lunch and a rest. I made my calendar available to all staff, but my blocked-out sessions did not give any detail. That was for me to know and me only.

Listen to your feelings too. Do you know how you are feeling? Do you know what is making you feel like you do? Do you know how to change a negative feeling into a positive? Learn to say no and ask yourself what you're going to do less of to make room for things that you say yes to.

If you can, create a time and place where you can be alone and turn off technology, both at work and at home. Each day make sure you do something for yourself, prepare a meal and tidy something up in your home. Find a pleasurable hobby or interest; being in the moment with a chosen activity will take your mind off other things.

What's the worst thing that can happen if I juggle all the time, you ask? On 15 March 2019 I was so busy that I did not notice that I was having a stroke. It was 2:20pm and I was calling some students to the office on the PA system. What I did not notice was that I couldn't pronounce their names properly. I was having a stroke and failed to recognise the warning signs. Lesson: take time for yourself. Have regular check-ups and listen to your body when it's telling you something is wrong. Stop in the moment and listen. Ask yourself when you last visited your GP for a physical.

'FAST test' to spot if you are having a stroke

F: Has your **face** drooped?

A: Can you lift your **arms**?

S: Is your **speech** slurred?

T: Call 000—**time** is critical!

Stress can happen at any moment. If not managed properly, it can infiltrate all areas of your life. Prolonged stress can generate long-term changes in the brain, causing issues such as anxiety and depression. Stress can shrink your brain. Research from Yale University revealed that chronic stress leads to a loss of synaptic connections between brain cells, which can in turn lead to decreased brain mass in the prefrontal cortex. The good news is we can avoid the negative effects of stress if we learn how to manage and reduce it.

Tips to determine whether you are too stressed

1. Mood swings: if you are moody, you could be suffering from stress. You might react to situations by crying at the drop of a hat.
2. Cognitive symptoms: stress affects our thinking, attention span, perception, focus, concentration, memory, sense of reason and problem-solving abilities. Making poor decisions is a good sign that you could be suffering from stress.
3. Eating habits: eating too much or losing your appetite can be two signs of stress.
4. Weight changes: your weight might fluctuate when you are stressed. This could mean weight gain or conversely weight loss from missed meals, busy schedules, poor food choices and not waiting to eat.
5. Physical sickness: muscle tension, headaches, rigidity and an increased heart rate are all signs of stress. Poorly managed stress can also lead to an array of other health problems such as skin irritation or a diminished immune system which makes a person susceptible to illness, infections and other conditions.

KINDNESS

A new Korean parent who had enrolled her children at my school asked me one day to help start her car. I grabbed a tea towel and a kettle of hot water and pretended to know what I was doing. I cleaned her battery, jiggled a few leads and got the engine started. She thought I was a mechanic as well as a principal! Winging it became an artform for me as a leader.

Several weeks later, I received a call from this woman's uncle. He turned out to be the South Korean ambassador to Australia and wanted to set up a sister-school relationship between my school and a school in the city of Gwangyang. I was not too sure at first, knowing nothing about sister schools or if the Victorian Department of Education would even allow it. The ambassador said he would pay for me and my staff to travel to South Korea and see the potential sister school first-hand before we signed any agreement. I flew with a teacher and the president of our school council. There I was in Business Class, listening to Celine Dion in my headphones singing 'I Am Alive', drinking my third cocktail and feeling on top of the world. Never in my wildest dreams could I have predicted being on that plane. The sister-school relationship went for several years. To think that it started with me pretending to be a mechanic!

I learnt that from small gestures of kindness come big opportunities. I also learnt that South Korea was a beautiful peaceful place, and that Business Class was the only way to travel.

KNOWING WHAT TO KNOW

My parents did not allow us to drink coffee or tea. One day I read that the local tennis club needed fresh players. I had heard stories about their afternoon teas. The scones, jam and cream were legendary. At 12 I asked my parents if I could join the tennis club. After pretending that I wanted to learn a new sport, I convinced them to let me join. I was a terrible tennis player, but I did not care. When that bell rang for afternoon tea, my face lit up. I would race to get my large cup of coffee and a couple of scones before scooping up the jam and cream and piling it on layer upon layer. I would then make a beeline to a spot where I could sit alone and savour every mouth-watering bite, grinning like a Cheshire cat. My mother would ask how I went at tennis, but I never could remember the scores. If she had asked me how the afternoon tea was, I would have been able to answer her with impeccable accuracy. Blueberry or raspberry!

I discovered that joining the club had lots of benefits—especially social ones—but was not so good for my waistline. Most importantly, however, I learnt that you needed to be able to play tennis to remain a member. This wasn't something that I could bluff my way through.

(I also learnt how to make scones. To this day, I love nothing better than a coffee with a muffin or scone by myself in a café. Somehow that Cheshire grin always returns when I take my first bite.)

Faking knowledge, skills and experience can only get you so far. To overcome a lack of knowledge, seek a source from which you can gather the information needed. I did a lot of professional development courses outside my area of expertise; I would read the agendas and minutes of meetings or committees I was not on, and I would talk to my colleagues about the issues that I was weakest in. I would use Edward De Bono's Six Thinking Hats mental model, especially the white hat signifying information-gathering (see 'Mental Models' for more detail). I sourced information from as many avenues as I could. I even once paid $14,000 to do the Good to Great Schools Australia program with the Queensland Education Leadership Institute (QELi). That course changed my whole outlook on getting what I wanted out of people. You must learn to use those in senior management or government, leveraging their roles and knowledge to assist your next step in change development. The more influential people you get to know, the greater your chance to learn.

KNOWLEDGE AND SKILLS

Behind every action is a conscious or unconscious thought. Most of the time we know what we are doing, and we know why. Sometimes we might just be going through the motions.

Not knowing what we are doing (or why we are doing it) is a disaster for a leader or for a teacher in front of a class. Students, staff and the school community deserve the best version of us as leaders. Being purposeful and present, genuine and empathic is being the best version of yourself. Know your own purpose, mission, vision, values and behavioural expectations, and know those of your workplace.

Purpose: why I do what I do? Why does my organisation do what it does?

Mission: how am I going to get there? My quest! How are we going to get there? Our quest!

Vision: what will the world look like when my purpose is realised? What will the organisation look like when our purpose is realised?

Values: what do I stand for? What do we stand for?

Behavioural expectations: how will I behave according to my values?

LADDERS

I am a firm believer in ladders. Not your everyday wooden or steel ladders, but the metaphorical ladders needed for leaders. However, it does not matter how many ladders you have if you do not know how to use them!

Ladder of inference

In our ever-changing environments, leaders are always under pressure to act quickly rather than spending time discussing and thinking through processes and facts. This rushed thinking can lead us to a wrong conclusion or a falling-out with other people. We need to make sure that our actions and decisions are founded in reality. When you accept a task, challenge or project, you need to be confident that everyone's input and reasoning is based on facts. The ladder of inference helps you achieve this.

Emotional intelligence helps us to become more aware of what we are thinking and feeling as we gather and analyse information. Inference refers to the process of arriving at a conclusion using reason or evidence, which is very important in school improvement and transformation.

The model was created in 1970 by organisational psychologist Chris Argyris and detailed in *The Fifth Discipline: The Art of Practice of the Learning Organization*, his 1992 collaboration with Peter M. Senge.

This ladder describes the thinking process that we go through, usually without realising it, to get from a fact to a decision or an action. The thinking stages can be seen as rungs on a ladder. I use this model during discussions, meetings, social interactions and projects as well as in my everyday life.

The thinking process according to the ladder of inference

Step 1. Observe the range of data you have before you

Step 2. Select data

Step 3. Add meaning to data

Step 4. Make assumptions based on meaning

Step 5. Draw conclusions

Step 6. Adopt beliefs based on conclusions

Step 7. Take action based on beliefs

Ladder of accountability

This ladder I used as a tool for assessing the current state of accountability for my school. Accountability has several levels. Some people climb to the top rung of the accountability ladder, while others tend to avoid accountability and cling to the bottom. The ladder itself explains the steps between powerlessness and achieving success. The bottom four rungs describe a victim mentality and the top four lead the way to accepting responsibility and becoming successful.

Accountability is essential for any school or organisation. Without it, it is difficult to get people to accept ownership of their actions because they believe they will not face any consequences.

When I noticed my staff showing a lack of accountability, I knew that it was not intentional but a sign that we needed to seek clarity by returning to our purpose, roles and responsibilities. Were we not clear enough? Were the role descriptions not detailed enough? Were they too wordy and not as simple as they should have been? Many times, I asked teams to contribute to their own role descriptions and determine how they related to our school context. When the staff took ownership of their accountability, I noticed that they felt valued and empowered.

Here are the rungs on the ladder of accountability. The place you want to be is at the top, so let's start there.

Climbing the ladder of accountability

Implement solutions: people here are all 'on board.' Whether or not they are the sole decision-maker, they assume responsibility for implementing their solutions and are committed to success.

Find/create solutions: people here own the problem and own the solution. They actively seek to implement solutions, and even if they cannot directly do it, they will work to move or support those who can.

Own it/take a position: people here own the problem and honour their commitments and responsibilities. They no longer make excuses or blame others.

Acknowledge reality: people here let go of magical thinking and acknowledge the reality of circumstances or events.

Wait and hope: people on this rung know that there is a problem that requires action, but they choose to stick their head in the sand in the hope that it will magically go away or improve without their input.

Excuses: people here avoid responsibility by claiming confusion or incompetence. They avoid tough situations, issues and challenges. These people want to be told what to do.

The bottom two rungs are **Blaming** and **Denial**... no further details needed!

Ladder of success

When we aim to reach a higher level, we are climbing the ladder of success. This ladder is used to represent a series of steps leading to a higher or better position. As you climb the ladder, you become more powerful, knowledgeable and successful.

I climbed the ladder of success despite my challenging upbringing. By working several part-time jobs while studying to become a teacher, I achieved my goal of paying my way. I made the decision during my teenage years to do better than my parents. I hated being poor. I hated not having what others had and I especially hated how some people treated me because I didn't have money. I had to study three to four hours in my Matriculation years to pass, compared to the other students who did one hour. Learning was not easy for me. I had to hear something several times before I could grasp it. I listened in class to the discussions and answers of other students to help me understand the text. I would deliberately be nice to the smart students just to take in their knowledge. I knew that I would be able to climb that ladder of success if I surrounded myself with friends like them. I owed it to myself to make the effort and better my chances in life.

I am especially thankful for my friends' families, many of whom invited me round for an evening meal. I missed my family when I moved into the hostel for girls, so being invited to my friends' homes made me feel welcomed and part of a real family. That was something I never forgot!

Tips for climbing the ladder of success

1. Decide and commit
2. Set goals
3. Be adaptable and flexible to changes
4. Be consistent
5. Always expect success
6. Take pride in your achievements, no matter how small
7. Thank others for their support and guidance
8. Know when you have achieved your goal, and then set another

LEADER AS ANTHROPOLOGIST

Honesty and confidentiality are critical to good leadership. Establishing the rules of engagement when you first meet people is critical and can often overcome issues that may arise later. Leaders must keep away from office drama, refrain from gossip and stay true to the values of honesty and integrity. Always make your intentions known, cover your tracks and avoid playing petty and unnecessary games.

When you deal in any kind of business, your word is all-important. It is your narrative. If you say you are going to do something, then do it. If you cannot achieve your goals, be upfront and speak up. If you have the right intentions, most of the time things will turn out right. If you have ulterior motives, your choices will eventually catch up with you. The consequences may be your downfall and the impact will have a ripple effect on others around you.

I wished some of my staff, especially my leadership team, were more honest with me was when I was a new principal. I had to rely on my instincts and, funnily enough, what I had learnt in anthropology studies during my Bachelor of Arts degree at La Trobe University! If nobody shares really important information about your new workplace culture, you end up flying blind. This is not what you want to be facing as a new leader. Anthropology teaches you to look for patterns when encountering new groups of people by analysing their interactions. In this way you can identify the pecking order. Listen to how people speak to each other. Observe their habits, their customs, their little idiosyncrasies. That was what I had to do at as a new principal. It did not take long for me to discover which people thought they were the leaders, as opposed to those who actually made the big decisions and led change and innovation. I realised that being a leader was not about your position or what you said, but about your relationships.

Learning to fake it to make it in my career as a leader came to me as a defensive method. I do not know how many times I would enter a meeting or walk into a situation where I was totally caught off guard. What is happening here? I would say to myself. I would stay calm, look around, listen, say nothing, observe the body language and read the play. I learnt this approach during my anthropology studies. When you do not understand a culture or language, you must study people's interactions, their gestures and especially their body language.

This approach of looking, listening and learning became a natural routine of mine, especially when I would enter uneasy or new situations. Saying nothing and trying not to put my foot in my mouth was more common sense than instinct for me as a leader. I was mindful when I entered these unknown situations to be always on guard. Following this rule of thumb in unknown circumstances gives you time to assess, think, decide and then react. As you become more confident with your leadership, you will realise that a leader doesn't always have to be in control and actively leading. You learn to use 'pause'-type behaviours, sit back and take it all in. Observe to understand the situation rather than to reply and intervene. Patience is indeed a virtue!

A true leader unlocks the potential of others to become the best versions of themselves. They inspire others to do their job properly and respectfully, and to enjoy it as well. A leader's actions should reflect their school's vision, mission and values. If you share your narrative with your staff, you must inspire them to follow you or your goals will never be realised. A leader makes a difference. The most important and vulnerable message you can share with your staff is yourself. Do not be shy!

LEADERSHIP STYLES

An effective leader motivates and inspires people to engage with purpose and vision. Leaders can be coaches and mentors who build an effective team where everyone can collectively achieve a vision. They can create and nurture other leaders. They have guts, are courageous and honest, and maintain a clear focus. They are strategic and strong with the technical aspects of their role and organisation. They are good at connecting with and empowering others.

I was often called upon to appear outwardly confident and committed to my purpose while taking leaps of faith. Sometimes I had to fake it to make it, but my intentions were always honourable and fair. If you can articulate and justify your thinking as a strategic leader, others will understand and follow. If you are dishonest and not transparent, you will not last long.

The essential qualities of a good leader are communication, vision, empathy, accountability and gratitude.

Here are the most common leadership styles according to psychologist Daniel Goleman. Each style works best in a different situation. Anyone can learn how to use these styles. Remember that they are meant to be used interchangeably depending on the needs of your team and the context.

The authoritative (visionary) leader

These inspiring leaders move people toward a common goal. Tell your team where they are going, but not how they can get there. Use this style when a school or organisation needs a new vision. I used it when I was appointed to a new position supervising a team more experienced than me.

The coaching leader

This style connects the purpose of the staff with the goals of the school. This style is empathic and encouraging and focuses on developing others for future success. When I used this style, I had in-depth conversations with teachers about how their goals matched with the school's purpose. This style established rapport and trust but did not work with some of my staff who required more direction and honest feedback. In those cases, I would use the coercive or pacesetting leadership styles.

To master the coaching style, you must learn how to engage in informal coaching and mentoring. You must also get to know the people in your team. When you know your people, you are better able to see where and when they need support and advice.

The affiliative leader

This leader promotes harmony within the team, encouraging inclusion and resolving conflict. To be good at this, you must value the emotions of others. This style can help resolve tension or conflict when trust has been broken and can be used to motivate people through a challenging time.

You will be required to focus on emotion to resolve conflict and remain optimistic. When the emotional needs of people have been met, they can then be ready to focus on the team's projects and goals.

The democratic leader

This style is collaborative, actively seeking input from teams through listening and conversation. I used this style when I needed my team to be on board with a new project with complete consensus. You do not use this with an inexperienced team who lack the necessary skills or with a team that isn't well informed about a situation. It is best to ask for input from team members who are motivated and knowledgeable with the necessary capability.

Get the whole team involved in problem-solving and decision-making. In some circumstances you must teach them the skills they need to do this. A good leader with this style must have active listening and facilitation skills. Set the situation up and allow the team members to talk through their options, then reach a consensus on what to do next. The GROW mental model is a valuable tool to use (see 'Mental Models').

The pacesetting leader

This leader focuses on performance and goals, expecting excellence from teams. Often you will need to jump in to redirect the discussion and make sure that goals are met. I used this style when I needed to keep a team on track. It is a way to nudge poor performers and still hold others to a high standard. While this can be a successful style, it can have a negative effect on the team and lead to burnout, exhaustion and high staff turnover. This works well when you need to get high-quality results from a motivated team quickly.

Everyone's motivation must be high. If you ask other team members to put in extra hours of work, you must be a role model and do the same.

The coercive (commanding) leader

These leaders use an autocratic approach relying on orders, total control and an understood threat of punishment. I would sometimes use this style when implementing new orders or change. Most of the time this style worked, but I did not like using it often because it risked having a profoundly negative effect on my staff, particularly when times were stressful.

I remember using this style to deal with a disease outbreak at my school. The commander style is best used in crisis situations, to accelerate fast-paced change and, in some cases, deal with problem staff.

You must be able to manage crises, think on your feet and make good decisions under pressure.

What good leaders should avoid

1. Telling others to do what they have not done themselves
2. Believing themselves the experts on everything
3. Thinking that they do not need any outside coaching and mentoring
4. Neglecting their own health and wellbeing
5. Defining success solely in tangible terms

6. Being selfish
7. Failing to inspire others
8. Failing to support others in tough or challenging times

Remember, people may not recall what you say—they will recall how you make them feel.

LEARNING PROCESS

Effective teaching is the biggest factor in determining student improvement across all areas of learning. Learning involves patience and time. There are six interactive components of the learning process: attention; memory; language; writing; higher-order thinking; and processing and organising. Teaching involves planning and preparation for learning; classroom management; delivery of instruction; monitoring and following up on assessment; family and community involvement; and professional development and responsibilities.

Good teachers create a positive culture of challenge and support aimed solely at improving their students' learning outcomes. They do this by making learning fun, planning according to the needs of their students and role-modelling the importance of learning. Using multiple sources of evidence to inform teaching and learning is critical. Good teachers use pedagogical approaches supported by evidence of effectiveness.

Literacy and numeracy skills underpin our ability to engage in learning, reach our full potential and participate in the community. Good teachers connect assessment with learning. They use assessment data to inform their teaching decisions, and curriculum standards to design and document relevant curriculum for their students. They promote the use of student voice and agency as a method of engaging children in their learning, developing their goals and revisiting them after each semester. They implement agreed school-wide practices to support student health and wellbeing.

Good teachers provide an inclusive environment for students with additional needs. They track the progress of students against the agreed standards. Schools and teachers do better when they encourage collaboration, a whole-child approach and trust-based responsibility with continuous improvement for their students.

When I took new parents around my schools, I knew which classrooms to go into and which to avoid. I felt awful that I had to avoid certain classrooms because, at the end of the day, I was responsible for what was going on. But it doesn't matter how many times you talk about good teaching and the importance of positive and fun learning environments: there are still some staff who remain 'beige'. I hated dull, boring and lifeless classrooms and worked diligently with teachers, teams and leaders to turn those learning environments around. It was always a work in progress and something that remained on my agenda as a leader. 'Average teachers get average results and outstanding teachers get outstanding results' was a mantra that I'd often repeat to my staff.

Good teachers seek to understand the learning needs of their students. Is this lesson content hitting their point of need? Have I audited their prior knowledge before I begin a new topic? Am I seeking feedback for future learning? Am I introducing the topic in the most creative way to excite my students? Am I making learning fun? Can I do better? Have I got the right resources? Do I even know what I am doing or am I simply going through the motions? Is near enough good enough for my students? Depending upon your answers, you are either on the right track to real learning or you are simply wasting your time and that of those you teach.

I was fortunate to lead Professional Learning Communities (PLCs) in my schools as principal. The work of the PLCs is characterised by a relentless focus on student learning. The active participation of teachers in learning communities leads to significant growth in professional knowledge, improves instructional practice and builds shared understandings of organisational values, beliefs and behaviours. The aim of PLCs is to increase teacher empowerment through collaborative processes and to promote a culture of collective efficacy and continuous learning through the research and inquiry process. It has been established that students' academic performance increases significantly over time when teachers participate in learning communities within schools and across networks.

Collaboration and communication between parents, teachers and the wider school community is vital to ensure the achievement of student learning goals and provide a positive school experience. All good leaders actively involve students and parents in the process of setting and assessing goals and reporting on student achievements.

I can remember a learning experience in my life that strongly affected me as a leader. Who throws a four-year-old into the deep end of a pool? My father, of course. He threw me and my five-year-old brother into a naval pool in Darwin because he wanted us to learn how to swim. That was the way he learnt as a child, so his children would learn the same way. Tough love, he often told us, was the best way to learn. We both went in, and we both came up. We were spluttering and gasping for air, grabbing at anything to breathe, but we both survived. I learnt not only how to swim but also exactly what tough love meant.

This lesson was to resurface (excuse the pun) many times throughout my career. Along with firmness and a commitment to making hard decisions, tough love is a daunting but necessary attribute for any leader. On many occasions I had to make exceedingly hard decisions as a teacher and principal. As leaders we must be able to think and make decisions on the spot. I was particularly good at that because I trusted my intuition. If it did not feel right, I would delay my response. My success rate was usually around 95 per cent. All leaders should allow a 5 – 10 per cent buffer for their decision-making processes. Always have a backup plan. I often wondered what my father's backup plan would have been had we not come up after he threw us into the pool!

LISTENING

I wished I had heard of Stephen Covey's *The 7 Habits of Highly Effective People* a lot earlier in my career. It is a definite must-read! Covey's fifth habit relates to listening: 'Seek first to understand, then to be understood'. I used to be quick with my verbal responses because that was what I thought a leader did. Wrong! I learnt that if I first listened to understand, then I would be better understood. Pausing is not a sign of weakness but of common sense. To check if my response felt right, I asked myself whether my head, hand and gut were aligned. If they were, then I went with it. If I was not too sure of my response or needed time, I would use my 'wise old owl routine' and sleep on it to return in time with my answer (see 'Routines'). There are three listening techniques that I used every single day in all my interactions with my students, staff and families.

Listening techniques

Empathic Listening. Empathy is the ability to understand and share the feelings of another, to imagine what they might be thinking. When someone had finished talking, I would reply: 'It feels like you are…?' The hardest part of empathic listening is that you must learn to separate other people's problems from your own. I had to set boundaries to take care of my mental health. This takes practice and is easier said than done.

Reflective Listening. This type of listening involves conveying to the other person that they are being heard and understood. When someone had finished talking, I would reply: 'And it sounds like you are feeling like that because…?'

Active Listening. This keeps you engaged with your conversation partner in a positive and genuine manner. Listen attentively as the other person speaks, paraphrasing and reflecting on what they say while withholding judgement and advice. When someone had finished talking, I would reply: 'And how can we help change that?'

MENTAL MODELS

I did not realise how important mental models were until I did mentorship training with the Victorian Academy of Teaching and Leadership.

A mental model is an explanation of thought processes. Mental models can help us shape our behaviours and problem-solving approaches. The following mental models saved my career. Knowing them, using them and understanding how they can solve those scary and sometimes out-of-left-field challenges is a necessity. I kept the template of the GROW model (my favourite and default) on my desk, ready to be used for any situation. The good thing about this model is that you can use it for all your interactions and plans, whether you are a leader or not. Once you have used these models in your work or personal life, they become second nature. If I can share anything with you it is to embrace one or several of these mental models. They can be applied to any situation or context in education.

GROW model

My favourite model, in case you missed it earlier.

G: What is the **goal** for this meeting? (What can I do for you?)

R: What is happening in **reality**? (In one sentence, what is the purpose of this meeting?)

O: What are the **options** to solve this problem? (What can we do?)

W: What is the **way forward**? (When shall we meet to review the situation?)

De Bono's Six Thinking Hats model

A good model to use when introducing something new. The coloured hats are a metaphor for directions of thinking. This could be used in a sequence to explore a problem, discussion or solution.

Blue hat: manages an overview of the process; summarises and decides which other hats to put on.

Green hat: demands creative effort and the consideration of different perspectives.

Red hat: allows for feelings and intuition to be introduced without need for external justification.

White hat: deals only in facts and figures, not arguments.

Yellow hat: seeks to identify the benefits of a scenario.

Black hat: critiques and imagines worst-case scenarios. To be used sparingly.

First-order and second-order change model

First-order change means that only small tweaks are required. I used this mental model when I had to tell my staff that the school was taking on a project that came from the Department of Education or our local region. I did not like changing plans midway through the year unless it was necessary. Saying 'tweaks' or 'small changes' was more likely to garner a positive response than words like 'major' or 'huge'.

Second-order change refers to major, mandated changes that need to be made to systems within a school. You will rarely meet with success by imposing change top-down onto staff, and I avoided doing that if I could. For a second-order change is to be successful, you must plan accordingly. You can lay the foundation for success! I would use De Bono's Six Thinking Hats for all second-order changes. That way everyone was involved and could take ownership.

Purpose, plan, picture, part model

You can use this simple method when introducing or re-establishing roles, responsibilities, strategic plans and so on.

1. What is the **purpose** of what we are doing or introducing?
2. What is our **plan** to achieve this?
3. What does it look like **visually**?
4. What **part** does everyone play?

Golden circle model (why, what, who, how)

1. **Why** are we doing this?
2. **What** needs to be done?
3. **Who** is doing what?
4. **How** will it be done?

Purpose, planning, programs, practice principles and professional development model (PPPPP)

1. What is the **purpose** of what we are doing?
2. What **planning** needs to be done?
3. What **programs** need to be designed or implemented to achieve the necessary and desired outcomes?
4. Which **practice principles** are being addressed?
5. What **professional learning or development** needs to take place to upskill everyone or to build teacher capabilities?

MENTORING

Mentoring is delivered by someone with skills and experience relevant to the mentee. The mentor is concerned with the development of their mentee. The mentee is expected to be responsible for their own learning, but a shared interest exists between mentor and mentee. When I mentor staff or other leaders, they select three goals that they would like to work on. A mentoring agreement outlines the process and timeframe involved. Principles of the mentoring process help guide and sustain the relationship, which is one of equality. The mentee will choose what to do, learn or ignore from the mentoring. Some results of the mentoring process are measurable, while others are not.

How can you be a good mentor?

1. Learn the techniques of good mentoring from significant role models
2. Maintain structure and reflect often upon your techniques
3. Adapt your focus to the needs of the mentee
4. Be organised and provide your mentee with an agenda and a summary
5. Use reflective notes
6. Understand the importance of a mentoring agreement signed by both mentor and mentee
7. Adhere to confidentiality
8. Make each session a positive one for both mentor and mentee

9. Maintain the tone of the relationship
10. Maintain progress
11. Set realistic expectations and do not expect too much from the mentee
12. Let the agenda flow
13. Avoid imposing your own agenda onto the mentee and process
14. Maintain the self-awareness to make better behavioural choices
15. Be humble and do not assume superiority
16. Do not project a state of dependency upon the mentee
17. Be aware of your own dependency as a mentor

A different kind of mentorship

At one point in my career, I needed to reapply for my principalship and had to resign to do so. Confusing, but that was what I had to do! I took three months off during the process of reapplying, interviewing and appointment. After seeing an advertisement for volunteers in the Herald Sun newspaper, I decided to apply. I trained as a mentor for the Victorian Association for the Care and Resettlement of Offenders (VACRO), which allowed me to support women in the Dame Phyllis Frost Centre prison. I mentored three women and enjoyed every single minute of it. When I visited the prison, I had to take off my jewellery and anything flashy. The women wear green jumpsuits, and visitors were discouraged from wearing similar colours. I went to the end-of-year concert and sat in the audience feeling immensely proud of the women, happy to be there supporting and encouraging them and sharing in their fun.

As a mentor, you are not to share aspects of your personal or professional life. Sometimes, though, paths inevitably cross. That night at the concert, I could have sworn that I saw several of my ex-students or their parents on stage! I would eventually like to go back to help develop programs to support women upon their release.

I learnt that there are many, many women in prison because of their relationships with men. Some women find refuge inside because they are away from the abuse. If you turned up on time and were reliable and genuine, they appreciated that more than anything.

Volunteering as a mentor has allowed me to connect with my local community and create a better future for my neighbours and those in need. Dedicating my time enables me to make connections, expand my network and strengthen bonds. I have met other volunteers and travelled within Australia and overseas to Denver, Vancouver and Seoul. Meeting people and listening to their stories has increased my sense of awareness and purpose.

MOTIVATION

As a teenager I worked part-time at Coles on the ice-cream machine and in the stationery, sock and ladies' fashion departments. I hated the sock department. It was boring! When the boss walked past, I pretended that I was rearranging, tidying and sorting socks. 'You're always busy, Deborah!' he would say. Bloody hell, I thought to myself. I was bored out of my brain, but I needed that job. One day my sister came in and stood by the socks. I blasted at her to go away. No, she replied, not until I gave her something for free. I thought about throwing a pair of socks at her but that would be stealing, and I was not going to do that, so I snarled at her and chased her away.

Working at Coles convinced me that socks are boring, but I learnt how to get my message across and rid myself of my troublesome sister. More importantly, however, the job taught me that appearing motivated is half the battle. In my career I came to master the art of motivating myself to listen and look enthusiastic through the most boring conference, session or workshop. Sit somewhere in the middle or on the aisle, so you can leave quietly or spread your legs to give yourself more room. Sit upright, seem interested and listen. If you get bored, take your thoughts somewhere else then come back. Use your notepad or laptop and write down your thoughts. Look up and show that you are still there. Smile and nod occasionally but sit still and try not to fall off your seat because you are bored out of your brain!

I had other part-time jobs growing up, and quickly learnt that dishwashers, babysitters and waitresses were considered to be at the bottom of the pecking order. At catering events I was hit on, ridiculed and at times scared for myself and the other girls. I particularly remember being at an all-male Christmas party. The only other woman there was the other young waitress. We were groped, laughed at and made the butt of several sexist jokes. I remember being frightened and saying so to the manager. He and several other men replied that I should have seen what they had done to the previous year's waitresses! As young as I was, I decided to take immediate control. I took the manager aside and said sternly and with conviction that if he did not put a stop to what was going on I was going to ring the police. We packed up quickly and left the premises straight after. I put a complaint into the agency that had sent us and said never send any woman to that workplace and that I would not work with that manager again.

This experience motivated me to treat people as I wanted to be treated. Whenever I was having a tough time at work in my later career, I would think back to my youth and remember the values driving my purpose.

There are two types of motivation: external (extrinsic) and internal (intrinsic). We learn as leaders when to alternate between the two. I could quickly identify staff who were self-motivated and those who needed to be motivated by external forces. In many professions it is often the desire for money that motivates people. This is not the case in education! Motivation is so important to those in education because of its crucial role in student learning. If you see a person who takes on greater responsibility, you will assume that they feel a greater sense of satisfaction and therefore work and commit harder. I tried as much as possible to foster teams to collaboratively solve problems and plan according to the needs of their students. I liked it when I saw our staff smile when they arrived at school. The staff lounge, for example, was designed so that there were comfortable couches, stools and high benches, tables for small groups and larger teams, flexible workstations, outside eating areas in a courtyard, a coffee machine, lots of greenery and positive and colourful surroundings. If the staff felt valued and supported, then they in turn would feel better motivated and this would pass onto their students. Did it work? Honestly, not all the time—but it did most of the time. You can lead a horse to water, but you cannot make it drink! No matter what you do for a small percentage of staff, you cannot change their disposition. That was always a work in progress.

NEGOTIABLES AND NON-NEGOTIABLES

Negotiables and non-negotiables follow your values and principles. They define not only what you will and will not accept from others, but what you will and will not accept from yourself.

It was the non-negotiables that I mostly worked with as a leader. I would not compromise on my daily routine and tasks. I would prepare my clothes the day before, shower and get dressed early each day, go over my tasks to be done, read the daily newspaper and have a good cup of coffee. These routines allowed me to be prepared and feel in control. I had the same expectations of my staff: be prepared, get to school on time, leave your personal issues at the gate, be open to change, be present for your students and plan according to their needs.

It was the same with my leadership team: there were expectations about behaviour and planning for students. One non-negotiable was a list of criteria in reading, writing and mathematics that all children had to meet in the school year to make sure that they were set up for success.

One thing you shouldn't compromise on is having an official lunch break to eat a proper meal, taking 30 minutes a day for exercise and giving your body time to reset ready for the next day. I should have been stricter on myself with this, as the first thing to go when you are busy is taking the time to rest and exercise. Now I am more in tune with my body and mind, and I think about how I want to feel each day. I make a list of five non-negotiables and follow through on them.

Five ideas for non-negotiables

1. Walk 30 minutes each day
2. Eat properly
3. Be kind to others
4. Be on-task and genuine
5. Sleep properly

I noticed that the better I became with my non-negotiable list and my expectations of others, the easier my life became. Reminding myself and others that certain issues were not on the table for discussion became my go-to method of dealing with challenging timelines, people and issues.

NETWORK AND NETWORK MORE

Throughout your upward rise you will meet many different people. If you want to make a difference in this world, you must learn how to use other people's roles to your advantage.

Actively going to conferences, meetings and get-togethers adds to your own knowledge bag. Listening to other people's points of view and understanding how they formed their opinions is a skill. You will develop your own theories and opinions, and networking can help with that.

I always treat new people I meet with respect. Here's a trick to remember names: let's say that Nancy always has a neat hairstyle: bookmark her in your head as Neat Nancy or NN. When you see her again, you will notice her neat hair and remember the nickname you gave her.

When at an event make sure to move around, make eye contact and chat to people. Be interested in their story. Ask questions to show that you're following what they're talking about. Always carry business cards and swap when necessary. You can do or wear something memorable so that people remember you—but make sure it's for the right reasons! Watch your alcohol consumption at work-related events.

I have learnt that even the most awkward moments can be turned around to become unforgettable for the right reasons. I was at a YMCA conference in Darwin and went downstairs for cocktail hour. I sat next to a representative from Hong Kong, and during our conversation we realised that we were both principals. I noticed while he was eating from a bowl of nuts that some of the shells were stuck on his chin. The shells remained there for some time and I was wondering whether to say something or not. I did not want him to be embarrassed, so I said he had something stuck on his chin and that it had been there for some time. He did not know what I meant, looking confused and unaware. So, being the gracious person that I was, I leaned in and with my fingers pulled the nut shells from his chin. Unfortunately, I could not flick them off, so was leaning in further and pulling harder when my surprise he screamed loudly in all sorts of pain. What I did not realise in the dimly lit foyer was that I had pulled the hairs from his mole on his chin! I slowly slunk away, foot in my mouth and face as red as a beetroot, to somewhere I could hide and take cover.

The funny thing about this embarrassment was that the man and I struck up a very meaningful relationship. After the conference we continued to remain in contact via email. He asked if a team of principals, leaders and teachers could visit me later on that year. I organised their trip to visit my school and one in Preston that had a bilingual Chinese program, as well as various universities and the head office of the Department of Education. I also arranged their accommodation in the city. When they came out to my school, I invited all of them around to my home and cooked dinner for them. In turn they invited me to visit Hong Kong the following year. On the quiet, I did notice that when my friend returned to visit with me, he must have shaved the mole or had the hairs removed! Being the ever-gracious host, I did not mention how we first met. But I must confess that I took the liberty to have a quick glance, when he was not looking at me, at his disappearing mole!

NO!

When I say no, I don't say it to be rude, selfish or disrespectful. Instead, I want to show that I'm on-task and assertive. When we are new in a position, we like to please. A new principal of mine said to me on my first day of teaching at his school: 'We do not like to make waves at this school, Deborah. Do you understand?' Oh my God! I thought to myself. What had he heard about me and how dared he speak to me like that? I didn't want to make waves but knew that I eventually would, so I told him that I understood. Play the game, Deborah! Be polite and respectful and bide your time. Eventually, that principal encouraged me to be the teacher and leader that I was. In fact, he became my best advocate. Thanks, Peter.

Being able to say no is empowering. I learnt to say no respectfully and maintain my relationships with others at the same time. Saying no helps you establish healthy boundaries and enables others to have clarity about what they can expect from you.

A leader cannot and should not say yes to everything: schools would be bankrupt, anarchy would reign, and everyone would experience stress, chaos and confusion. Being clear, honest and open while saying no allowed me to alleviate frustration and burnout.

A leader who frequently has to say no in a respectful way can cultivate healthy relationships. A staff member once said to me that she liked my leadership style because if someone asked me a question I would either say no, yes, or that I would get back to them! I did not actually realise that I was doing this, because to me it was about being open and transparent. I was later to discover that the staff at that school had not previously had a leader who answered their concerns so quickly and honestly.

Saying no to children is easy. As behaviourist Bill Rogers says: just say no, and if the student carries on or becomes defiant, say no again. Stand your ground, keep your eyes on the student, be firm but fair and restate the instruction. This became my best disciplinary technique.

OPENNESS

Being open to innovative ideas and new learnings is important for any aspiring leader. However, I learnt through experience that there are times to be open and there are times to be guarded. Being too open and showing all your cards can lead to disaster. Be especially aware of this when meeting new people. Always play your cards properly. New leaders should hold back a little, learn and take things slowly at first. Talk to as many people as you can, audit current practice and improve your contextual understanding; then you can be more open. Ask lots of questions when you want to learn something. Look for hard tangible evidence and do not just listen to someone's opinion. Words are words. Look at actions and body language. Take your time and do not rush into making decisions too early. When you do feel confident, be more open and honest. Once you get to that position do not go backwards. Stay true to yourself, your values and your openness.

OPTIMISM

We all know the saying 'you only live once'. After surviving breast cancer, a stroke, a tumour on my thyroid and a suspected hole in my heart I realised this was not exactly true. A quote that more deeply resonates with me is 'we live every day and die once'.

Quotes mean a lot to me; they help with my daily affirmations and purpose, and give me hope for the future. I am an audio-visual learner, as are many people, and I look for meaning and purpose in life with quotes and visual images. Daily affirmations, cards, trinkets and photos are there to remind me to be grateful, to enjoy every day and always look for the positive. I do not mix with negative or narcissistic people, preferring to walk away rather than bother to confront them. I aim to always surround myself with happy, half-glass-full people. I have come to believe that this growth mindset is necessary and immensely powerful if I want to live longer and enjoy the life ahead of me. I set myself small, specific goals and targets every day and celebrate each one. Even the smallest of milestones is a reason to celebrate.

I am now enjoying coaching and mentoring leaders in education and the corporate world, and running professional development workshops. I am also volunteering my time working with VACRO to design training modules for women re-entering the workforce from prison. I talk to people in prison about schooling, education and their children. I assist others with their career and life journeys. When people say that I should slow down and smell the roses, I tell them it is my story, and I am going to write it. Who is the author of your story?

ORGANISATION

Organisation is necessary for any leader. Leadership requires us to put things into a logical order and to take an efficient and orderly approach to tasks and projects. Cleaning up your desk, office or filing system contributes to a healthy and productive workplace. Once the small stuff is organised, the big stuff is a lot easier to handle.

Being organised allows us to preserve our energy and personality by separating different aspects of our lives. My house from the street looks neat, tidy and colour coordinated. The back of the house is where you will find the true Deborah. My patio is a calming environment full of ferns, colour and coolness. At work, my office has a desk with formal seating in front. Behind the desk I have family photos, trinkets and collectables from my travels to provide me with calm and comfort. Until I reflected on it, I did not realise how similar my home and work environments were. I soon realised that they reflected the dual aspects of my personality. My work environment said that I was formal, in control and outgoing. My home environment catered to the quiet, calm and introverted side of me. Being accessible with an open-door policy put me very much in the public domain at work. A survey into principal's roles found that they had an average of 40 interactions per hour at school. It is no wonder that I was quiet, reserved and loved my own company when I got home.

PASSION

I consider myself blessed to have a sustained passion for teaching. Passion was the fuel in the fire that guided me through my 46 sometimes challenging years in education. When you have passion for something, it shows. I could identify the passionate teachers by the way they appeared to live, breathe and love what they did. Their passion could be felt and seen in the way they went about their day-to-day duties and interacted with their students. If you do not have passion, you might as well be flying blind. I am glad that I started as a 21-year-old teacher and finished 46 years later with the same passion in my body.

Teaching is not for everyone, and as a young woman I had very different ambitions. My father said to me: 'Why don't you become a teacher instead of doing economics and politics at university?' In those days (yes, back in the olden days!) women had two career choices: teaching or nursing. Well, I hated blood so that left teaching. I replied to my father: 'Dad, I do not like kids!' I wanted to go into politics and become a premier or even the prime minister. Aim for the stars and I might reach the roof was what I told myself. Unfortunately, my social sciences teacher at school scored my last essay before Matriculation exams a crippling 44 out of 100. He said that I needed to work harder if I was going to pass. Little did he realise how hard that failure would hit my chances of graduating with the score I needed. I changed my preferences and applied for the following courses in the event that I passed:

1. Teaching at Melbourne State Teachers College
2. Town planning at RMIT Melbourne
3. Economics and politics at La Trobe University

I was accepted into Melbourne State Teachers College as a physical education major. At 24 years of age, I then began my BA at La Trobe University just to get back at that teacher who had failed me in high school and show him that I was better than his 44/100 score.

I am glad that I went into teaching, but it is not for everyone. You must love children, have a passion for making a difference and be willing to put in the hard hours and work that is needed. My own daughter would have made a fabulous teacher, but she did not do well in exams and consequently became a childcare worker. I could tell who on my staff was at school to make a difference and who simply clocked on to get their money. Passionate teachers inspire and genuinely get the desired outcomes that we all aim for.

I learnt as a leader that you can have a team of champions, but that does not mean you have a champion team. Everyone has a purpose. We all have strengths in certain areas and skills that we can use or share with others. The trick is to find out what your strengths are, match these with a passion for doing something and—as a bonus—get paid for it. Good career advice and listening to others can lead you down pathways that you never would have imagined. Be creative, take those surveys to match your strengths and passions, and go for it. Embrace risk and don't be pressured to do something because your parents said to do it. Choose your career path wisely, because you are the one who has to wake up every day and turn up. Your goal, as I have said, is to get paid to do something that you are good at and enjoy.

PLANNING

A plan requires you to decide what you want to do, followed by a formulation of what you're going to do. As a leader I often had to make decisions on the hop, while at other times I could allow myself to think and plan. My better decisions were made when I used what I called my 'wise old owl' routine and gave myself time to think through a proposal (see 'Routines'). Knowing your plan and being able to articulate it to others is especially important for leaders. I lived by the rule that prior planning prevents poor performance. This means you need to research the topic, talk to others, look at different models and doing your due diligence before you can get it right in your own head. Yes, you can build the plane as it flies, but better to know what the plane might look like and whether it's sturdy enough to make the distance!

PERSISTENCE

Persistence is an important quality that teachers must model to their students. Repeat your efforts, change your strategy, capitalise on momentum, reset, look at the bigger picture, reward yourself and keep optimistic. Persistent students, teachers and leaders have a vision in mind that motivates and drives them. Highly persistent people are often thinkers, dreamers and visionaries who see their lives as having a higher purpose. Their vision keeps them focused and they usually display great emotion and energy.

Stay true to your goals, identify your purpose, select a suitable mental model and track its journey. Use a calendar, diary or vision board in your office and or home to remind yourself of when you'll celebrate. I surrounded my office with photos of my family, trinkets from my students, cards of appreciation, colourful images, happy quotes, graphs and a calendar of events to remind me what needed to be done. I also had these on my computer, phone and tablet. If I needed to recharge, I went laterally and gave myself permission to reset or to chill out for a set period. If I do not look after myself, how can I look after others? Besides, I make better decisions when I am happy, positive and healthy.

Ways to stay on track

1. Get a mentor or coach
2. Have the support of colleagues
3. Be in healthy relationships in your personal life
4. Ask for help from your leader and those within your team
5. Have something to aspire to
6. Celebrate and party when your goal has been achieved

PRINCIPAL

Effective principals nurture a safe and purposeful learning environment that promotes constructive and respectful relationships with all members of the school community. They must be advocates for students, promote positive relationships and develop individual and collective efficacy to optimise learning outcomes and wellbeing. To do this, you will need highly-developed interpersonal and communication skills supported by outstanding emotional intelligence. This ability to connect with and understand others enables us to feel, use, communicate, recognise, learn from and manage our emotions and the experiences of those around us.

For me, being a principal was an honour and a privilege. It took me 14 applications and eight interviews to get my first school, but I got there. Effective leaders lead by example and I was not going to give up. While there were many good times, there were also many learning curves. I remember someone once saying to me that being a principal was a glamorous job! I almost choked when she said that to me. Was she joking? Was she for real? Upon reflection I could see where she was coming from. I got to wear power suits, colour-coordinated clothing and good jewellery. I drove a nice car. I always had my hair groomed and make up on. But she did not see me putting my hand down the toilet to retrieve flushed lunches, wiping faeces off the walls of the toilet, cleaning the urinals, mopping vomit off the floor, changing the clothing on children who had soiled themselves, getting balls off the roof, capturing and securing a Rottweiler running loose in the school yard, or (more often than I like to admit) disarming an aggressive student or parent. Glamorous, no. Ever-changing, yes!

As a principal, I learnt...

- Not all referees are trustworthy when you interview prospective staff
- Take the time to select the right staff
- Do not be pressured into making a rash decision
- Ask pertinent questions when seeking a reference, especially the questions no one asks
- Don't go to school alone late at night
- Check rolls and staff lists manually, as errors can cost money
- Have a healthy work/life balance
- Check in with your feelings and body when they're trying to tell you something
- Not everyone will like you: it's lonely at the top!
- You are damned if you do and damned if you don't
- Keep updated on current educational practices
- Seek advice and support from your colleagues
- You'll have approximately 40 interactions per hour, so think on your feet
- Work smarter, not harder
- Listen and talk to the entire school community
- Organisation is a must
- Get the right tools for you to do your job effectively
- Be surrounded by loyal co-workers

As a teacher, I learnt...

- Students must be at the heart of every decision
- Not to take your spouse to every work function
- Have a class gift policy, because someone always misses out
- Remember who you sit next to at functions
- Not to drink or embarrass myself at a function
- Have a karaoke song at the ready when called upon

- Not to collect balls off a roof
- Not to tell anyone I have a bus licence
- Be careful what I write in my work program
- Never make a mistake with money or numbers
- Not to hide the pet mouse in the classroom cupboard and forget about it
- Never call out the principal or boss in public
- Be mindful of playing games
- Stay out of drama and gossip
- Stay away from drama kings, queens, princes and princesses
- If you are going to vent, do it alone and outside of school
- Do your research and due diligence
- Leave your personal problems at the gate

PRIORITISING

I had only just started my first appointment as a principal when I had to drum up the courage to speak to my staff about the first agenda item for our weekly meeting: *teabag in the wrong bin*.

What the bloody hell, I thought to myself. I had been in education for some years and at 41 was considered incredibly young, inexperienced and raw for a new principal. Making it even more interesting, I was female and taking on a school with declining enrolments and an imminent threat of closure. A school where the biggest item of concern at a staff meeting was teabag disposal!

A difficult school with declining enrolments did not deter me. I loved a challenge. I knew that if anyone could turn around a failing school, it was me. As my mother often said, I had more front than Myer. Indeed, the school went from 160 to 420 enrolments in my six years as principal and entered the top 10 per cent of high-performing schools in the eastern region. Not bad for someone born to alcoholic parents, someone who had lived in 14 different places including the Housing Commission flats! Now, back to that staff meeting.

Seeing the teabag item on that agenda was one of the things that made me decide I wanted to write a book. Surely this was not what educators studied and worked so hard for? Why not discuss how we could go about spending the $4 million school budget? What about looking at our data on student learning outcomes? Or finding ways to lessen the number of students performing at the lower end of the scale and improve the students at the top end? No, instead we were to spend time talking about the critical matter of who put a tea bag in the wrong bin! That was obviously more important than elevated expectations and achieving our key improvement targets.

I can remember that meeting like it was yesterday. I was fired up and I let it rip. I discussed the importance and purpose of staff meetings, saying that we only met once a week and needed to prioritise our agenda items from most to least important. I asked who wrote the agenda item in question. A staff member who was passionate about sustainability and doing the right thing spoke up. I decided to listen with the intent to understand. In this way I let the fishing line go out, and reeled it in when I had had enough. From now on, I said, we will deal with menial items at another time. Besides, just put the bloody teabag in the right bin everyone! Do we need to have a referendum to settle the issue?

I was soon to realise that 95 per cent of my time as a leader would be spent dealing with 10 per cent of the school population. Principals spend many hours on trivial issues, and we often do not have the time we need to prioritise the significant issues in our schools. As you read my story, you may remember the illnesses that I came to experience 20 years later. This was another lesson: I failed to prioritise my health. Why did I not notice the warning signs? Why did I not notice the continual impact of dealing with school issues from 6am to 10pm at night, and the dire consequences to my health that nearly killed me? Without prioritising our health, we cannot prioritise our work.

PURPOSE

A sense of purpose reduces anxiety, improves sleep and overall health, and helps people cope with setbacks and disappointments. Without purpose, resilience can be hard to find. Purpose also helps with social connections and a sense of belonging. When people are empowered to turn their purpose into action, anything is possible.

Tips for finding your purpose

1. Find your passion: what are you good at? What are your strengths? What do you love to do? What is your ideal job?
2. Think about what you want your life to be: something that you enjoy, have a passion for, are good at and can get paid for.
3. Write it down: what do I want to do? How will I go about it?
4. Plan: how am I going to get this dream job? What qualifications do I need? How will I fund my studies or training? Do I need support? What do I need to know? What don't I know and how can I get the information that I need?
5. Activate the plan and use the GROW model: what is my goal? What is happening in reality? What are my options? What is my way forward?

Just do it! Start your progress and get moving.

QUIRKY

I love working with quirky, different, eccentric and out-of-the-box personalities. As a leader I looked for these people to complement my leadership teams. People with these personality types act differently and look at the world through a unique lens. They often think abstractly and have random thoughts. You combine these people with linear rational thinkers, and you have the perfect team. I was a linear rational thinker, but I did not want to surround myself with likeminded people. I knew my strengths and weakness as a leader, and a good leader looks for others to counterbalance these areas to achieve the best team. A tremendously successful team values each member's opinions and thoughts. Egos are put aside, and the collective efficacy of the team that works collaboratively gets the best results.

QUOTES

Quotes inspire. I think of my favourite quotes when I have to write something or when I am facing a challenging situation. A simple quote refocuses my thoughts and helps me remember what is important in an instant. Using other people's words gives me perspective. Sometimes it even challenges me, giving me courage and determination when I need it most. Focusing on specific words or phrases in a quote gave me direction and clarity in my role as a leader. I have even made up a few of my own quotes as well.

My top self-talk quotes

1. GOMO, GOPO and GO#O (the latter only to be used under extreme circumstances!)
    a. GOMO: get over it and move on
    a. GOPO: as my mother would often say to those she could not stand being around, get over it and piss off!
    a. GO#O: now that I am retired, I can say this in my head and only with those I absolutely cannot stand
2. Purpose, vision, mission and values
3. Prior planning prevents poor performance (PPPPP)
4. Keep it simple, stupid! (KISS)
5. A caring teacher touches many hearts
6. Everyone has the right of reply: if you hear or see something that involves you, you have the right to go to the person responsible and ask for an explanation.
7. Excuse vs explanation: when people respond to a question or are speaking about their behaviour, it can be either an excuse or an explanation. Learn to tell the difference!
8. No surprises: never tell your staff do to something with no notice or order them to comply. This leads to dysfunction and distrust. Better desired outcomes can be achieved with preparation and transparency.
9. Buy in, block or bow out! Buy in to our school goals, block everything we propose or bow out and get out of this school.

10. Pivot on one foot and do a turn-around, or protect yourself and don't do anything
11. Ego means that you either fear change or are just plain silly and cannot comprehend what is being proposed
12. Use the Eisenhower Matrix for making decisions about what to do:
    a. If it is important and urgent, do it first
    b. If it is important but not urgent, do it next
    c. If it is urgent but not important, delegate
    d. If it is not urgent and not important, do not do it
13. Avoid negative people and situations

3 Rs: RESET, REFOCUS AND REPURPOSE

Resetting one's purpose or pathway in life is like resetting an alarm. We can do this with aspects of our personal life including relationships, finances or even accommodation. We can also use it in our professional life regarding our career path, study choices, role or responsibilities. A reset clears any pending errors and brings a system to normal condition in a controlled manner.

Refocusing changes our emphasis or direction. Busy people can do this by practicing meditation and focusing on breathing.

Repurposing is the use of something for a new purpose by modifying it in some way. I used to surround myself with pleasant visuals in my school and home offices. I would have trinkets that I collected from my various travels near me and inspiring quotes above my desk. If my mind wandered, I would look at them and they would make me feel happy, inspire me and make my thinking more settled.

While we feel good after achieving a goal or target, the feeling is not sustainable. It is imperative to always be learning and growing in life to achieve happiness that is lasting. Make the following tips into habits that will keep you from feeling bored or stuck.

Tips for resetting, refocusing and repurposing

1. Imagine the year ahead. Close your eyes and imagine yourself in the future. What are you doing? Where are you? Who are you with? How are you feeling?
2. Where do you start? What are your goals? Do what will make you happy and stop worrying about others. Choose forward-thinking goals.
3. When will you start? Today, tomorrow, next week or when? Visualise where you want to be and how you want to improve.
4. Decide when you will check in with yourself and reflect on your progress.
5. How will you use language when speaking to yourself to stay focused? Your thinking voice should resemble that of a motivator.
6. Keep a daily journal or to-do list. Ticking off tasks will assist with accountability. This is a habit that can keep you committed to your goals and help you assess your progress.
7. Be specific with your goals so that they are measurable. Letting someone know your goals can enable them to assist you when you are achieving them, but also to be there for you on your down days.
8. Call a mentor, coach or friend to support you.
9. Have short-term, medium-term and long-term goals.
10. Take a good look at your goals and do not try to do too much. Who can help you and what resources do you need? This about the possible blockers to success and what you will do when you reach these road bumps.
11. Celebrate your successes. If you do not celebrate, then the whole quest is pointless.
12. Do more of the things that make you happy. Challenge yourself and move out of your comfort zone.
13. Remember that it is a process. Enjoy the ride and do not focus on the destination too much.

RELATIONSHIPS

There are four types of relationships: family, friends, acquaintances and romantic relationships. For a relationship to be healthy you must have empathy, communication and commitment. My best relationships were based on honesty, openness and mutual support. I always established the rules of engagement beforehand. In leadership, establishing relationships with colleagues is especially important. In fact, it saved my life on several occasions. Being a principal can be a very lonely position and it is important to establish true, honest relationships with others. You never know when you will need support, and I always offered support in times of need.

To have good relationships you must have effective communication skills. You need to be able to talk to students, staff, parents, tradespeople, suppliers, contractors, lawyers, politicians, justice system personnel and others.

I had an assistant principal who always reminded me that our roles were about relationships, relationships, relationships! Val, you were always right. (For more about Val, see 'Students'.)

RESUME

You put on your resume the skills you will demonstrate in the position for which you are applying. The skills you choose to highlight will show your potential employer if you have what it takes to succeed. Writing a resume and addressing the selection criteria can be made simpler by following this formula.

Resume formula

D + E + O = R

Definition + examples + outcome = upon reflection

Define and write in your own words what the selection criteria mean. What examples can you show to prove that you have the right skills and knowledge? What were the outcomes? Lastly, reflect upon whether you would have done anything differently. List all the skills that you have. Find all the skills required for the position that you are applying for. Tailor your skills to the position. Keep in mind how this workplace would benefit by selecting you as the successful applicant.

Useful skills and attributes

- Leadership
- Time-management
- Problem-solving
- Flexibility
- Communication and negotiation
- Teamwork
- Creativity
- Confidence
- Positivity
- Responsibility
- Decision-making

- Mindset and attitude
- Adaptability
- Emotional intelligence
- Active listening
- Organisation

In teaching, it is also good to demonstrate how you can analyse data. Interpreting sets of data helps schools understand growth and progress. It is a good way to show that you can demonstrate and interpret. Writing is invaluable in any profession, but especially as a teacher or leader. Similarly, typing skills are always useful. Knowing another language is great, so add this if you have the skills. Most positions nowadays require at least a basic level of technology proficiency.

Another thing: make sure you have the right address of the school! Visiting a prospective workplace is always a clever idea. Get onto their website and learn as much as you can about them. What is unique to that school?

Make sure to have both female and male referees. You want people who can attest to your skills and good character. Give them a copy of your application and let them know in advance if you get an interview.

You may have to try several times to get a position, but remember this Japanese saying: 'you fall seven times, but you get up eight'.

ROLES AND RESPONSIBILITIES

We all have distinct roles, some of which we are given whether we like them or not. Mine were wife, mother, principal, volunteer, sister and daughter. No one can give all these roles equal amounts of time and attention, so we rotate in and out of them daily. Sometimes we do them well and sometimes we neglect them. When at work, be at work; when at home, be at home. Be present in whatever role you are doing, and do it well. Sometimes we need to give ourselves pep talks. Hello, you're doing an excellent job! Hello, you need to be home tonight and miss the drinks after work to be with your family! Do not be sad because you changed track or feel obligated. When the chips are down, it is our family members who are there to pick us up. Invest your time with them wisely.

ROUTINES

I love a good routine. Here are a number of different routines for you to consider.

Old Mother Hubbard routine

My father was often away in the navy for weeks at a time. My mother would make do with extraordinarily little, and she relied on our grandparents for additional money to support our weekly expenses. It never ceased to surprise me how my mother would go to the cupboard and there would be one crinkled carrot, an onion, a couple of potatoes and some pearl barley. She would methodically cut and grate the vegetables and make the best-smelling soup every time.

You do not need a lot of ingredients to make something worthwhile come to fruition. What made my mother's pots of soup taste so good were not so much the ingredients but the love that went into them. Nonetheless, that soup taught me an important lesson: always have an emergency fund, supply or means to exist. Plan always and have the ability to pay your own way.

You may not have all the answers, but you need a bag of tricks and tools to reach into when difficult situations arise. I call this my Old Mother Hubbard routine. I have always believed that in our mind we bookmark memories, and from these memories come pearls of wisdom. Things we may have subconsciously heard, seen or read can come to the front of our minds in the most unusual settings and at the most opportune times. I was particularly good at this, and so was not fazed with difficult problems or conversations. I could rely on two outcomes: either I was going to put my foot into my mouth, or I would come out with something that was exactly right to settle the issue, defuse the situation and leave everyone happy!

Wise Old Owl routine

I used this when I needed time to think about a decision I had made, or wanted to speak further with someone before I made my decision public. I would sleep on it overnight. If I woke up in the morning with my decision confirmed, then I went with it. You do not always have to decide straight away. Giving yourself time to think will allow your brain to fully process your subconscious thoughts.

Flight Path routine

One day I was on a flight to Sydney. The captain announced that we would be flying at 32,000 feet and would stay at this height for a period before descending. Flying at 32,000 feet and staying on course became an analogy for me as a principal. If I could work at that level, then I could get to my goals and targets as planned! I also applied this aviation thinking to my school teams. Let's figure out where we are to go, fly at a productive level (not too low and not too high) and we can reach our destination. I used this language often in my meetings. It is important to know if you and your team are flying too low by being unproductive, or flying too high by being over-productive and working too fast and too hard. Being over-productive can lead to burnout and an unsustainable level of expectation. Flying at 32,000 feet safely will lead to your desired outcomes being achieved.

Curve of Life routine

Using a curve to guide our career and plans is useful for leaders: we start low and work our way up and over. However, when we reach our peak, it is important to know when to start a new venture, relationship, project or career move before things go south. Most of my career moves or changes were made around the five-year mark. I started at a new school, worked my way up, achieved my goals and targets and then found that I would get bored and needed another challenge. I wanted to be stimulated so that I could continue to learn, grow and make an impact in education. When things are going well, one feels happy and challenged. When I was not feeling that way, I knew that it was time for me to move schools and begin a new curve of life!

Poker Face routine

Someone once said to me, 'You are a thinker, Deborah.' I was surprised by this statement and asked the person why she had said it. She told me it was because my face stayed still and motionless. I wanted to laugh out loud but restrained myself. I was not a thinker; I was bored out of my head. Upon reflection, I called this my Poker Face routine. When I was bored or lacked interest, I would just sit there and not move or comment. It became a favourite routine of mine because it worked!

Recipe routine

You can lead a horse to water, but you cannot make it drink. There are some people who cannot think or decide for themselves. They need to be given a recipe or a script to follow. I could identify the people who needed recipes given to them, and off they would go to get the job done. I admired others who could think for themselves and create their own solutions. Some people are 'recipe' types and others are more creative. They can all contribute to a productive work environment.

Chaos routine

This routine is one of reorganisation: it requires you to throw everything up in the air, spill all positions and write new job descriptions, expectations and systemic procedures. When you throw everything up in the air, it can create chaos. I did this quite a lot as an experienced leader, but it is not a routine for new leaders, for whom it could go horribly wrong. Spilling leadership positions and opening them up to all is risky, but for me it created a new team and a new direction.

This is an extremely tricky routine to pull off. Very few leaders have successfully done it and stayed around to explain. You really need to have done your homework to understand a school's culture, systemic organisation, workforce structure and staff. I used this routine when I went in as the principal of an exceptionally large school. In my interview I said that I would go in carefully, audit existing practice and then slowly implement change. Well, I lied. To be fair, I genuinely meant it. But what I saw, heard and felt during my first few days at that school did not sit well with me. The school needed immediate intervention and I had to do something or my credibility as a leader would go down the plug hole. Role descriptions and staff responsibilities needed urgent attention. Everybody complains, but during this process you get to see the real personalities. You see those who want to buy in and those who want to block. Then of course there are those who do not do anything and choose the option of bowing out. Cultural change can take years. Your focus is on building a culture that is positive and consistent in achieving outcomes. I managed to survive and pull it off.

Nodding Syndrome routine

I came to notice that when I spoke at a meeting, some people would nod their heads. Were they nodding in approval or just going through the motions? We are taught that to show you understand what a speaker is saying by nodding your head. But that is not the case for everyone. Some nod simply because they nod to everything as a matter of routine. Did they understand what I was saying? Did they get the meaning of my presentation? Some people only nod sometimes, and others do not nod at all! The more time I spent in leadership, the more I noticed people nodding just for the sake of it. It does not always mean that they agree with you or that they have even accepted what you are saying. Nodding does not mean acceptance; in fact, it could mean the total opposite. Be careful of those who nod in public but in private do their own thing. Do not be fooled! Reading body language is an art and a skill for leaders to learn.

SELF-CARE

After putting on weight throughout the years after having had two children, I decided to focus on my health and lose some of that excess fat. It took six months. I lost 17 kilos and looked a million dollars. I went to the gym several times a week and ate a healthier diet. This was the year we established our sister school relationship with South Korea. The year was going swimmingly until November. I noticed a lump in my left breast and went to get it checked out on Christmas Eve. I had let it go for six weeks before I made this appointment. The doctor looked me straight in the eye and said: 'Are you ready for this? You have breast cancer!' He then sent me for an ultrasound and to an oncologist on that same day. My life changed in that split second. Over the following months I had a lumpectomy operation, radiation therapy for six weeks and chemotherapy for six months. I only took six weeks off from full-time work as a principal during my radiation treatment, but continued working while having chemotherapy every second week for six months. It was a nightmare.

The second unwelcome event happened seven years later in March 2019: I had a stroke at school. I had rung my husband on the way home after hitting a few roadside kerbs and said that I was not feeling well. 'Have a bath,' he replied in his usual non-committal style. Instead, I did what any sane person would when confronted with the unknown: I asked Siri how one knew if one was having a stroke. I realised that my tongue was hanging halfway out of my mouth, and I was lisping. Alone at home, I rang for an ambulance and ended up in the Royal Melbourne Hospital that night. The CT scan confirmed that I had in fact had a stroke. But more was yet to come: when I revisited the stroke unit in June, an MRI picked up on a six-centimetre tumour on my thyroid that needed surgery. The doctors also thought I might have a hole in my heart, and organised umpteen tests.

With that news, I knew that something needed to change in my life. I could not take the risk of another stroke, so I focused on looking after my physical and mental wellbeing and did not return to school. After 10 months away from the pressure-cooker environment, I decided to relinquish my principal position and retire.

I learnt that one can only dodge so many bullets in a lifetime. If you do not look after your health, it will look after you. I also learnt that my work/life balance was uncoordinated, and that my wellbeing was now more important that full-time work. I did not want to have any regrets in my life, and I had to find a new meaning and purpose if I was to move forward with the next chapter.

The lesson: always look after your health. Exercise regularly, no matter your age or schedule. Moderation is the key to everything. To keep a healthy mind and body, make sure that both are coordinated. Be connected to nature. Bring plants inside your home or redo your garden. Stay internally motivated and always look for the positive aspect or the unseen benefit. If you need further help, seek professional assistance and find out where support groups meet. Have regular medical check-ups and hold your GP accountable. It is worthwhile to invest in a good health insurance fund that includes hospital and extras. Similarly, remember to keep up your ambulance membership!

STAFF

In a school you won't just find leaders and teachers: you'll also find education support staff, administrators, cleaners, unpaid volunteers and gardening and maintenance staff. All have different Enterprise Bargaining Agreements (EBAs) and follow different standards and regulations. Leaders need to know Human Resources requirements and regulations, and keep up with the latest EBA changes. This is not easy, as they change every four years. Give yourself time to understand and interpret the changes that will affect your school policies and procedures. Develop a close network of colleagues and attend the forums run by the Australian Principals Federation (APF). A highly skilled business manager is as asset in any school, as they deal with most HR issues and fiscal management. Get the right staff to run your school. Sometimes this means reshuffling staff, hiring new staff and letting others go. That's what leaders have to do. If you settle for anything less, the consequences will not be good.

Teachers are, of course, at the heart of the school. However, I have found that leaders who encourage a mindset of superiority will only create a culture divided between teachers and other staff. I did not care if you were a teacher, educational support staff or the gardener: every single member of our school community was equally valued, listened to and respected. Each single member had a role and set of responsibilities, and together we aimed to achieve our school's purpose, mission and vision. They say it takes a village to raise a child, and schools are not different.

We lived by our agreed values and behaved accordingly for the betterment of all. We understood our school's strategic plan and could articulate why, when, where and how we went about our day-to-day routines. The values of respect, responsibility, honesty and trust, care and compassion, teamwork and personal best permeated our school. That is what makes an organisation work best: everyone being on the same page. I now carry those values over into my mentoring and coaching.

When selecting staff for your leadership team, you aim to get the best. I was fortunate to work with some of the best educators in the system. We were all vastly different in knowledge, skills and thinking, but our moral purpose was for our students. They came first in all our decisions and planning. The leaders who did not put their students first were overturned or replaced.

Not all teachers are suited to the role; some lack interest or expertise, while others have more serious problems such as addiction or mental illness. I do believe that people can change their ways and be better versions of themselves. That takes time, commitment and arduous work. Counselling, coaching and mentoring is often the best course of action. Some people are unfortunately hampered by denial, fear or ego. Denial is quite common: it's someone else's problem, not mine! Then there's fear of being caught, fear of being wrong and fear of admitting a problem. Ego gets in the way when people think of themselves as untouchable. On many occasions I had to initiate hard conversations to hold these staff accountable. The GROW model (see 'Mental Models') and unsatisfactory performance processes and guidelines are especially useful in these instances. Your school's legal unit and Department of Education conduct and ethics branch are great supports. If you are a leader, you must challenge inappropriate behaviour. The best outcomes for your students should be your reason for stepping up and taking action

STUDENTS

The world we live in now is quite different from the world not long past. Our role as educators is to empower students for the future. As leaders, our role is to empower our teachers to teach students to be critical thinkers and problem-solvers.

Student voice needs to be a focus for all schools. Students with a keen sense of agency work harder, have greater focus and interest, are less likely to give up, are better at planning, are more likely to choose challenging tasks, set higher goals and have improved concentration when facing difficulties.

I always like to encourage and build a culture where teachers and students work together, where the young voices of our future are heard and valued. That way all stakeholders in our school community are on the same page and have an equal share in the direction of the school's purpose, mission, vision and goals.

I always encouraged my staff to think of every student as their own child. The important ingredient in any school is finding, supporting and developing exceptional teachers.

Student management

If you cannot control a class of students as a teacher, then you are in serious trouble. We want to minimise disruptions to learning. Start small: handle one child, then two, then a small group and then move onto larger groups. Learn their learning styles, habits, preferences, backgrounds and what works for them. Be playful but firm. Be in control and fair. Set boundaries and expectations of acceptable behaviour. Challenge them and make learning fun. Get to know everything about them, where they were according to assessment before they entered your class. As a teacher you are to add value to their learning with a minimum of 12 months' growth. If they are below their expected level, it is our role as educators to improve them. It will be hard, especially if they are six or 12 months behind, but a good teacher does not give up. We must try all avenues to get students up to speed. I saw throughout my career some outstanding teachers who completely turned around a child in their class. Ask for help and seek advice if you don't know what to do. Treat every child as if they are your own and never give up.

Some teachers couldn't believe how I could get the most disruptive student to stop what they were doing and to follow me. I was known as the 'student whisperer'. I would go up to the child, crouch down to their level, and quietly say the following lines:

> *I am going to stand up and turn around, you are going to come quietly behind me and we're going to go to a place where we can talk quietly. You are going to follow me out of this room and if you don't then I am going to lift you up and carry you out myself! Do you like Milo and chocolate biscuits? Let's go to the staffroom and make a cuppa and get some biscuits. If you don't come quietly with me, then I am going to go to my office and ring your mum and dad and they will come up to get you.*

The last line always worked!

I have been working lately in a secondary school with Year 7-10 teachers and students. It amazes me how many teachers these days want to be their students' friend. I highly advise against this approach. It does not work until you have the respect and trust of the students, and that takes a long time. Set the ground rules of class behaviour, of what is acceptable and what is not. High expectations and high student learning outcomes go hand in hand. I once wrote an article listing 20 things to do before you ever yell at a student. Having great lesson starters and plans and meeting students at their point of need is a must. Get up from your seat and walk around the classroom, being actively involved with and—more importantly—available to your students. Crouch down to their level and don't talk over them. Get side by side if they are extremely sensitive, and then move on to face-to-face. Show them that you like them and genuinely care about them. Get them to write their learning goals, and track progress together to keep them informed and committed. Celebrate their successes.

Student management is crucial for school leaders. I would suggest that a starting point is to audit current practice at your school. What is the model in use? Why was it introduced? Is it being used by everyone in the school? Does everyone know the purpose of the model and its expectations of them? Is the model relevant today in your school? If you walked around the school, what evidence would you see of the model working or not working? Does the model require first- or second-order change? Do staff need a refresher? Is everyone on board? How are you using student feedback to inform you as to whether the current model is relevant? What do you keep? What do you get rid of? What do you introduce? What do you change completely?

Younger students need assistance with their self-regulation. By Grade 2, a child should know the difference between right and wrong and be able to self-regulate. I would work especially hard with students in Prep and Grades 1-2 by talking with them about good choices, values and acceptable behaviour. If I gave a 'time out' to a student, I would make sure that I spent some time with them afterwards when they were in a better frame of mind to talk about their triggers and how to make better choices. Children of all ages will make mistakes and test boundaries. Knowing the stages of child development when teaching enables you to understand the causes of their behaviour and will help you respond appropriately. You cannot apply the same method of discipline to a Prep student and a Grade 6 student.

They say that a Year 7 student new to a school can tell after only three days which teachers are good and which are not. Students know who likes them and who does not. Teachers who stand side by side with their students instead of at the front of the classroom are more readily accepted.

For many years I was lucky to work with Val Brittain, an assistant principal who never labelled or judged students who misbehaved. She looked beyond their behaviours and tried to work out what was causing them to be so disengaged. What were their triggers? Val investigated their backgrounds, personal and academic histories, relationships and interactions with others. On many occasions she completely turned these unwilling students around. We need more teachers like Val in our schools.

When you go to audit student-management practices at your school, I suggest using the PPPPP model (see 'Mental Models'). What is the purpose of the audit? What is the plan? How do you picture it? What part does everyone play? I recommend checking out the Berry Street Education Model for auditing current practices. The following are my suggestions for a comprehensive audit aiming to build student success.

Areas for investigation

1. School
2. Relationships
3. Stamina, endurance and pace
4. Engagement
5. Character

School

Build school-wide procedures that improve flow, rhythms and body regulation through focus on physical and emotional regulation and de-escalation of the stress response.

1. Build a curriculum that promotes academic performance, wellbeing and future pathways
2. Acknowledge trauma where it is known
3. Create opportunities for students to self-regulate
4. Better student teacher relationships enabling:
   a. Co-regulation of emotions, reactivity and impulses
   b. Self-regulation of emotions, reactivity and impulses
5. Make predictable and known timetables for lessons (what happens when the teacher is away should also be known in advance)
6. Create opportunities for mindful practices at various times of the day

Relationships

Increase relational capacities in staff and students through attachment and attunement principles: create bonds that enable people to tune into one another's emotional states. Build specific relationship strategies for students who are difficult to engage.

1. Build relationships
2. Create a foundation of safety, tolerance and respect
3. Teach personal resilience and self-regulation
4. Teach social and emotional intelligence
5. Demonstrate the values of friendship and teamwork
6. Deliver strategies to build lasting, strong relationships by improving and demonstrating positivity

Stamina, endurance and pace

For tips on building up these strengths, see 'Energy and Stamina'.

1. Create a strong and sustainable whole-school culture of independence in academic work by nurturing resilience and emotional intelligence

2. Remember: stamina increases and improves attention, concentration and the management of distractions
3. Consider the structure and availability of support groups
4. Encourage a growth mindset for academic learning and achievement
5. Develop a passion for learning, getting it done, persistence and following through

Engagement

Establish and embed engagement strategies that build willingness in students who are experiencing difficulties.

1. Understand the pathways to complete engagement through flow activities
2. Increase opportunities for active engagement: flexible timetabling, hands-on activities, multiple learning models, etc.
3. Broaden, build and savour positive emotions
4. Build motivation through fun and healthy play
5. Ignite curiosity and interest through real-world applications, vocational pathways, problem-solving and investigation

Character

Harness an approach based on values and character strengths to enable student success. Self-knowledge leads to empowered future pathways.

1. Help students articulate their own values, purpose and vision
2. Find personal meaning in those values and extend that meaning to include others
3. Understand oneself and others in the context of culture and community
4. Identify personal strengths and practice those strengths
5. Explore strengths through narratives, stories and role models
6. Cultivate attunement through tolerance and respect for the character strengths of others
7. Understand inclusion and diversity as they apply to your school demographics
8. Understand and employ character strengths for future pathways

SUICIDE

It was a quiet Sunday afternoon in the high-rise flats in Fitzroy. After a big weekend of drinking, Sundays were often an enjoyable time in our family. My mother would be in the kitchen cooking and my father sitting at the table reading the paper while drinking his beer. My brother would be out and my sisters would be at home with me. This day, my mother asked me to go down the shop to buy some tomato sauce. We were having roast pork. As I was skipping back to our block of flats, I heard an almighty thud. I looked around and got the shock of my life. It was an image I still remember to this day. I saw that someone all in black had jumped from somewhere above and was lying there motionless on the ground. My reaction was instantaneous. I screamed, dropped the sauce and ran to the lift, back up to the 20th floor. We later heard that a nun had jumped from the 16th floor. Suicides were common in the flats, as were drug-dealing, alcoholism, assaults and rapes.

Suicide happens all too often. Observe the moods of your friends, family and colleagues. Check up on them when something doesn't seem right. Remember that we need to listen with the intent to understand rather than to reply. If people need more encouragement than you can give them, urge them to seek professional help. We must all walk together with those in need, then let them walk alone when they are ready.

Several colleagues of mine committed suicide. Their decisions were influenced by a range of factors: heavy workloads, legal issues, complaining parents, a lack of support, difficult students, difficult colleagues, elevated expectations. One teacher went into his school on a Sunday, tidied up his desk and completed all his tasks, drove to the beach and killed himself. He was a beautiful, caring and gentle man. The person whose suicide affected me the most was a close colleague. He was a truly knowledgeable, skilled and talented educator who was driven to despair from a lack of support and the enormous pressures of his principal job. Families, colleagues and school communities are left to try to understand why things were so bad that these people took their own lives. As we all know, some questions never get answered.

TEACHERS

How does one go from a shy child who disliked reading, writing and public speaking to a successful author, mentor, motivational public speaker and leader of one of the largest government primary schools in Victoria?

I can see myself, small and shy with bushy blonde hair and freckles the size of boulders, in a Grade 6 classroom at a Catholic school in regional Victoria. There I was, standing with a book in hand and the teacher demanding that I read a paragraph. Knees trembling, palms sweating and my heart ready to explode, I froze. I could not get a word to come out of my mouth. I could see the word on the page, and it was 'lift'. *The young boy with a bouquet of flowers went into the lift to visit his mother who was having a baby in hospital.* The word was lift! That was all I had to say, the word lift. But I could not. I could not get it out of my mouth. The teacher threatened that the whole class would stay in at recess. She thought that I was being defiant, but I was anything but defiant.

My classmates were sniggering and hissing behind me, urging me to say the word. After what seemed like a lifetime, the teacher dismissed the class and told us all to get outside. That one single experience continued to traumatise me throughout my secondary school years until I found a caring and compassionate English teacher in Year 12. He changed my attitude toward reading, writing and speaking in front of large groups. You do not include verbs in your sentences Deborah, he told me. From that moment on I met with him after school, and he tutored me with my writing and encouraged me to read more often. One caring, patient teacher changed my career path.

TOUGH TIMES

Moderation is the key to everything. Understanding our triggers in life and the way we react to situations is paramount to the success of all human decisions and interactions. We have our flaws, but knowing them is key. When tough times come, deal with what you can control and seek help for what you can't control. Just one foot in front of the other.

Everybody goes through tough times. Acknowledging what we are going through is the first step toward improvement. As teachers, we learn to look for signs in our students. It is also important to recognise the signs in our peers, acquaintances and family members.

Throughout my career I met people who sounded confident but had anxiety or depression. Others looked healthy but felt horrible. Then there are those who are quite attractive but have incredibly low self-esteem. I have realised that every single person is fighting some sort of battle, dilemma or issue that we know nothing about. When in doubt, be kind: it costs nothing and can achieve so much.

The signs that someone is going through a tough time can vary. Has there been a change in their behaviour? They might not be taking care of themselves. Are their relationships good? Do they prefer to be alone? Are they unresponsive? Do they have difficulty sitting still or resting? Of course, they may simply present as anxious and worried.

What can you do? Ask them how you can provide support. Check in with them as often as you can. Encourage them to talk about they are feeling and to seek help. Do what you can to help them with healthy eating, sleeping and exercise.

When I had the stroke and stopped work, I felt very much alone and out of control. I cried all the time and thought that I was going to have another stroke, end up wheelchair-bound and in an aged-care facility. But, as with my breast cancer, I survived. I got into bike riding as an outlet and rode for miles around bike tracks. It was my escape. When I had the stroke, I walked two kilometres a day, then eventually five kilometres per day. I found Victoria Park in Echuca particularly spiritual with its view of the Murray River. Back home in Bundoora, I discovered the walking tracks around the Darebin River. Flora and fauna are the best remedies to promote mental and physical wellbeing. The only downfall to walking is meeting the occasional looney tune on the tracks. I always armed myself with a bum bag filled with tissues, umbrella, phone and personal alarm just in case!

As a leader, you will need to take care of your wellbeing so that you're ready to face any tough times that may crop up at school. Believe me, they will happen when you least expect them!

One day, an anonymous person contacted my primary school and asked to speak to the principal. I got many of these requests each day. Hello, how can I help you? I asked. The reply was not what I expected. The stranger claimed that there was a bomb in the school! That was my signal to get out the emergency procedures clipboard and head into action. Another day, a brown paper lunch-order bag was found in the corridor just before morning recess with a note saying that the school was going to blow up! Thankfully, these were both false alarms.

On another day, parts of the roof collapsed and narrowly missed students. Within 15 minutes a news helicopter was circling the school, four television stations were waiting outside the front gate and five ambulances were lined up to take the injured to hospital. I quickly grabbed my trusty clipboard to make me look important, put my glasses on and marched straight out to greet the reporters. I had no bloody idea what I was going to say but I was convinced that once I was there the right words would come out of my mouth. Yes, I said, we are putting safety of the students first; we have cleared the area and now waiting for a risk assessment officer to come. All our emergency procedures have worked and we are now liaising with the parents of the five injured students, with the Education Department and the Minister already having been contacted. 3AW radio announcer Neil Mitchell saw the interview and rang the following day to speak to me. After the interview he told his listeners that Principal Deborah Patterson was fantastic. She knew what to do and how to speak to everyone involved. She obviously knew her procedures, and he wished that all school principals were like her! I remember feeling so proud. My 'look important' props had worked, I had said all the right words and I was a star! Well, for one day at least.

That was a fake-it-to-make-it situation. I was helped by my proficiency in the art of looking professional, and by using key words and language suitable for the interview. Plus, as ever, I had more front than Myer!

Be prepared for anything and always have a simple script ready. If you are interviewed, be wary of the media because you could be taken out of context. Keep your replies simple and in line with official statements. You can also contact the media unit within your organisation to seek advice.

Life is full of tough times. It is how we pick ourselves up that matters. These are the experiences from which we learn the most.

TOXICITY

As a principal I was accustomed to people coming into my office, sending me an email or ringing to voice their concerns. I always welcomed feedback, but often had to deal with people who were angry, dysfunctional or even dangerous. I am often asked what to do when receiving feedback that is not given in a polite manner. That depends on your strength and stamina, and on the tools in your toolkit for handling difficult conversations. If your resilience tank is low, then find an alternative way of dealing with the issue. This could mean a blocked-out time in your calendar, a 'Not Available' sign or a blind drawn on your office door. Give yourself space and time (mental and physical) until you are ready to face the person or the issue. When you are ready, have a plan of attack and use the GROW model: what is the purpose of the feedback? What is happening? What options do I put in place for a resolution? Which way forward?

Do not think that I was always a perfectly well-spoken leader. When necessary, I was prepared to tell parents that I was happy to support their children's enrolment at another school! I would not tolerate parents who were out to get a teacher fired. Leaders must back our staff. At the same time, we also have an obligation to support our school's parent community. It is a juggling act.

Listen with the intent to understand, acknowledge what is being said, seek a resolution with options and try to shut the discussion down as soon as possible. Drawing issues out, repeating mistakes and brushing people off will only exacerbate the situation. When I could not get through to some parents, I gave them the phone number of the Education Department's regional office. As leaders we're sometimes tempted to pass the buck, but unfortunately cannot. We must be pillars of respect and promote positive relationships. The more situations I dealt with, the better I became at conflict resolution. Practice makes perfect!

If we work around toxic people, we risk accepting their behaviour as the norm. Watch out: toxic people make others toxic. The more I dealt with these types, the more I learnt from then. I would observe and make notes to myself. When you peel away the layers of these people, you begin to learn what makes them tick. You can do this by listening, understanding and acknowledging without compromising your values. Sometimes, however, I threw that routine out the door! Don't let people waste your time if they are not open to mediation.

Only confront toxic people when you have built their trust. My motto is that I'm not going to talk behind your back, I'm just going to say it to your face! If I was dealing with someone especially toxic, I would ask them how they were going to fix the issue. If I wanted to be supportive, I would ask how *we* were going to fix it.

With skill, you can turn a potentially toxic interaction into a positive one. There was a mother at one of my schools. She was the parent whom most teachers avoided. I, on the other hand, found her to be very genuine, slightly controlling, anxious at times and someone who loved her children above anyone else in her life. One day she barged into my office without any notice. She was angry with one of the teachers and wanted to let me know about it and get me to 'fix' it. I immediately went to my mental model toolkit and pulled out an imaginary copy of Stephen Covey's *7 Habits of Highly Effective People*. Covey's fourth habit is 'Think Win-Win'. I wanted to win with my outcome, and the mother in my office wanted to leave feeling as if she had won. Both of us ended up achieving our goals. As she was exiting my office, I said: 'Now come on, put your big girl panties on and get on with it'. I did not know where those words came from. The assistant principal in the next office heard me and could not believe that I had made such a comment. She said only I could get away with saying something like that!

Even if you are a skilled negotiator, you cannot turn around all toxic interactions. I had to invoke the trespass offence several times as a principal. First there was a mother who threatened me while she grabbed her son's tub of books out of my hands, breaking my glasses and a bone in my little finger. Then there was another mother who called me everything under the sun beginning with the 'F' word. There was the father who wanted to rearrange my face. There was the student from a neighbouring secondary school who told me to suck a part of his body! Last of all were two parents who texted me abusive messages when they found my mobile number. I remember getting the notifications while I was at a Christmas breakup celebration for principals. Ping! Ping! Went my phone for a total of 10 texts. Of course, I read them. They were so vile and demeaning that I left the celebrations, drove back to my school and rang the Education Department's legal unit. I had to spend the next three days writing a letter of response to the Department outlining all the events involving the family. This matter sat with me all during my holiday break, and my headspace was consumed by it the entire time.

A positive outcome to this story is that the family left our school and enrolled at another outside my network. I was later to find out that they caused the same chaos at their new school. Unfortunately for principals and teachers, these issues are increasing. Many parents think that they can come into a school and blame everyone else for their issues. Even more annoyingly, they ring the regional office or write a letter to the premier, and then the principal gets rung up or emailed with a 'please explain'. Most of those parents have issues and get a buzz out of causing unrest at the school. Instead of being able to say what I really wanted to say, I had to be polite and uphold the values of integrity and respect.

Not everyone has the same definition of toxicity: one parent rang my school and asked if I could tell her whether the glitter that we used in classrooms was toxin-free. I was already dealing with self-harming Grade 6 students and a fraudulent Facebook account being used to bully and threaten, and this parent wanted to know if my bloody glitter was free of toxins! I had initially asked her to repeat the question, thinking that the office had relayed an incorrect message. How did I reply when I heard her answer? Was I polite and respectful? Did I adhere to the Department of Education's values of integrity and respect? No! I politely lost it. I explained in a very civil voice that I had more pressing and urgent issues to deal with than answer her question, and that I was going to hang up because I was very, very busy. What did she do? She rang the regional representative and lodged a complaint. The next day the regional representative contacted me to convene a meeting to mediate and apologise. Toxic can have more than one meaning for school leaders...

UNDER PRESSURE

The ability to work under pressure involves dealing with constraints that are often outside your control—these might be resource or time constraints, difficult tasks or unforeseen changes. Sometimes I performed better under pressure, but in the end it was unsustainable. Pressure hinders the key faculties we need to perform at our best: judgement, decision-making, attention and emotional management. I kept the saying 'calm in a crisis' in the back of my mind when I encountered some of my more difficult issues.

Tips for performing under pressure

1. Take a deep breath: breathing deeply and slowly triggers the body to stop releasing stress hormones and start to relax
2. Always focus on the positives of the situation
3. Stay eating heathy foods and sleeping properly

4. Surround yourself with positive people
5. Take some time to think about the situation that you are facing
6. Stay in tune with your feelings when in the situation: understanding how you are feeling in the moment is a positive step
7. Assess the situation
8. Break the tasks down
9. Use the Eisenhower Matrix for making decisions about what to do:
    a. If it is important and urgent, do it first
    a. If it is important but not urgent, do it next
    a. If it is urgent but not important, delegate
    a. If it is not urgent and not important, do not do it
10. Do not procrastinate
11. Take action

UNSATISFACTORY PERFORMANCE

Unsatisfactory performance is the repeated failure of an employee to perform their duties in a manner expected because of negligence, inefficiency or incompetence. I had to handle several staff performance issues and used the following method.

Tips for managing unsatisfactory staff performance

1. Be specific with facts
2. Collect multiple pieces of evidence
3. Have a professional and personal performance plan agreed upon by both parties
4. Know the needs of your employees
5. Create clear expectations of job performance
6. Have a confident, values-driven mindset
7. Follow departmental guidelines and recommendations to the letter
8. Seek legal advice if in doubt at any stage
9. Document everything and keep a paper trail

10. Focus on feedback
11. Ask questions, listen and understand
12. Hold one-on-one meetings
13. If in doubt, always have someone else present to record as a witness
14. Provide support where necessary

Leading a school is never easy. No matter how competent the school leadership team, there will always be some problems with performance. Teams face a lot of issues that add up to mediocre outputs. Disengagement is a common cause of poor performance.

The biggest drivers of disengagement

1. Not having the right knowledge, skills or attitude
2. A lack of motivation
3. Personal problems
4. Team disagreements
5. Not being the right fit

It isn't fair on the team when someone is underperforming. A leader needs to intervene and, in some cases, begin unsatisfactory performance processes. These conversations are often the hardest to have, but as a leader you must equip yourself for them.

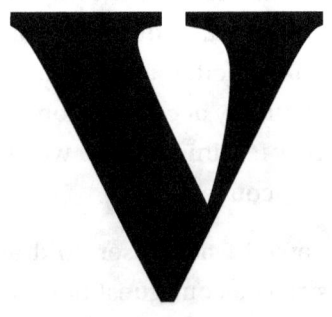

VALUES

I once taught in a team-teaching scenario with a colleague named Malcolm who always asked me to consider the values that were important to our students, to the way we taught and to our wider school community. I had just taken on a position of responsibility and was too busy at the time to fully appreciate his question. It wasn't until he died and I went on to more senior positions that I truly understood what he was asking.

Values support standards of behaviour. They represent our judgement of what is important in life. After Malcolm died, his wife came my school two days a week to rewrite our values in cooperation with the students, staff and parents. I wanted Malcolm's legacy to live on at my school. Our values were respect and responsibility, honesty and trust, care and compassion, personal best and teamwork. We then decided on the behaviours that would go with each value. We wrote a school dedication incorporating these values into our everyday lives, a dedication recited at the weekly assemblies to this day. Vale, Malcolm.

VANCOUVER, OR HOW TO ENJOY YOURSELF IN A STRANGE SETTING

When in an unknown social setting, do not be afraid to just get up and have fun. I was attending a YMCA conference in Vancouver and stayed on a couple of days to visit some schools. On the last night, I decided to go into town to buy some souvenirs and do a pub crawl. I have learnt that the Aussie accent gets lots of unsolicited attention, free drinks included, and that people like to talk to you. My accent was once described by a stranger on a visit to the USA as 'very feminine'. Not a word I would use to describe myself! Anyway, back to Vancouver.

In one bar on my pub crawl, I was chosen to draw raffle prizes: here we have an Aussie from Australia as our guest of honour! I played along with the routine and scored lots of friends. I finally ended up at the bar of the hotel where I was staying. It was a cold, rainy Tuesday night. I like talking to people, connecting with them and learning about their lives. At this bar I quickly worked out that I was in for a long night. To my left was a 36-year-old man who had been married to a woman for a year but was miserable and drowning his sorrows because he did not know how to tell her that he was gay. To my right was a father of four meeting his girlfriend before he went home to his wife and children. To my far right was a photographer named Randy, whom I remembered from the conference. Opposite me were two women who were open, loud and proud. It was like a scene out of Cheers. They all reminded me that they had heard how Aussies liked to have a fun time. Then my ears pricked up! 'Achy Breaky Heart' by Billy Ray Cyrus was playing on the radio. I called out to all line up and follow me. Up! Up! There I was leading the entire bar in a line-dancing routine. We were loud, we were singing, and we rocked that joint that night. We all downed several shots before closing time. I promised them that I would show them a fun time if they ever came to Australia. It was the most unbelievable, memorable experience that I've ever had.

I learnt to just go for it and not be afraid to make a fool of myself or have fun. I learnt to listen, to have empathy for others and to be grateful.

Tips for being ready in an unknown social situation

- Have a favourite song handy: you never know when you'll need to perform
- Memorise some good dance moves
- Always know how much alcohol you have consumed, and stay in control
- Stop drinking when you start to slur your words or miss your dance steps

VISION

A vision statement in education is a public declaration about what the school hopes to achieve if they successfully fulfil their purpose or mission. By outlining what the school is trying to achieve, all the stakeholders in the school community—teachers, administrators, students and families—can work together in a common direction toward growth. A vision is a guide for creating plans, setting goals and objectives, making decisions and coordinating and evaluating the work on any project. A vision helps keep schools focused and united, especially with complex projects and in challenging and stressful times.

Sample vision statement

(School Name) is a school that provides young people with the opportunity to be innovative, creative and passionate about learning while developing a strong sense of community and global responsibility.

Sample mission statement

(School Name) aims to provide an educational experience that will not simply prepare students for future job pathways, but will also stimulate them to see possibilities for innovation and inspire them to create their own unique opportunities through further education, training or business enterprises.

VOICE

Vocal projection is the skill of using your voice powerfully and clearly. It is a technique used by teachers to command respect and attention. All teachers must learn to how to use their voice.

Know your focus. To whom are you speaking? Use the space or room that you are in to project your voice. Speak with confidence and clarity. Learn how to hold the attention of your audience and help your message better resonate with them.

Stand tall, clear your airways and breathe properly. Speaking too softly, mumbling or talking too fast can distort your message. If you do not talk to people very often, your voice may grow weak from lack of use. Being clear with words helps your projection. Being soft-spoken is not a bad thing, but teachers need to talk at a louder volume so that students can hear the important things that are being said.

A good speaking voice is pitched low rather than high, and is resonant rather than flat and monotonous. Yelling and shouting can cause your voice to jam up.

The six elements of vocal variety

1. Volume (loudness)
2. Pitch (high or low)
3. Pace (rate)
4. Pause (silence)
5. Resonance (timbre)
6. Intonation (rise and fall)

Teachers need to avoid using the extremes of their vocal range, as yelling and shouting can cause voice stress. Practice good breathing techniques when singing or talking. Support your voice with deep breaths from the chest and do not rely on your throat alone. When you are tired, your throat feels tight or it hurts to talk, you may have vocal strain cause by muscle tightness.

Our tone, pitch, inflection and quality of articulation deliver subtle messages about the kind of person we are. They convey our thinking, mood and feelings at any given moment.

Tips to prepare yourself for classroom, stage or public speaking

1. Know your audience
2. Give your full attention to your audience's engagement
3. Have a plan: beginning, message and conclusion
4. Be aware of your appearance and body language
5. Be expressive and do not be afraid to use humour (make sure the jokes are tasteful!)
6. Speak with passion and commitment, and know your content
7. Show the audience that you care for them and share in this moment with them

You are there to influence your audience, so know your purpose and how you will deliver the message to create a meaningful encounter.

Having a voice in the metaphorical sense means that you have the right or power to influence or decide about a particular topic. Our voice is the medium through which we communicate our ideas, emotions and personality. A leader needs to use their voice to convey passion, guts, determination and excitement. Our voice can convey anything: a feeling, a place, an idea. A leader must use their voice to create change. People need to be inspired.

A leader must stay cool, keep our feelings intact and deliver messages over and over in our daily conversations. Speak with intent, stand tall and know your content. Show passion when needed and do not get sidetracked. Everyone is entitled to their own opinions, and strong feelings usually come attached to those opinions. I used humour to break the ice in intense settings, but mostly my voice was clear, direct and loud enough for all to hear.

When I was an assistant principal, my principal told me to find a boy who had run away. It was 40 degrees outside, and he was down the back of the oval on top of the cricket nets. I was in high heels, and I was bloody hot. I stood at the top of the oval some 50 metres from the nets and shouted to him at the top of my voice. GET OFF THE NETS AND GET HERE! I pointed to my shoes. He did not move. I repeated myself. GET HERE NOW! I turned around and walked back to the office praying that I would not have to repeat myself. Unbelievably, he followed me like a lamb. I learnt the importance of projection, firmness, short messages and knowing my audience. I do have to at times refrain from using this disciplinary technique with my husband!

VOLUNTEERING

I walked into a meeting between a parent and our school's business manager. The parent stopped talking, looked at me and asked if I wanted to join the local YMCA Whittlesea Board as a volunteer. What did it involve? Only one hour-long meeting a month. I could do that, so I said yes. The following year I became the president of that board, and, several years later, a director on the national YMCA Australia Board. I was on the Governance and Licensing Sub-Committee, and was Chair of the National Redress Committee for one year. I was fortunate to travel to Canada, the USA and Korea as a representative for the Y. Volunteering and giving time to non-profit organisations who give back to the young people and local communities is extremely rewarding. I adhere to the saying 'give more than you take'. This quote aligns with my purpose in life: giving back to my community and supporting those less fortunate than myself.

WARDROBE

What you wear to work or to an interview can often add to or hinder a favourable outcome. This is also something interesting for teachers to consider: I found that boys often preferred brighter colours: reds, blues, oranges and yellows. Girls often preferred the softer, subtle nurturing pastel pinks, creams and greys. I would wear darker, more cooperate colours for my formal meetings and softer colours for my mediation meetings.

WOMEN

When I was 15, I had a part-time job in a news agency. One day the owner told me a joke. How can you tell which is the male bird? I said I did not know. The one who flies the highest in the cage, he replied with a funny, creepy grin on his face. I just giggled and went about my business. When I got home, I told the joke to my parents. They were not amused. They looked at each other with the strangest of expressions and my father said to my brother, come with me! They both went straight to the newsagent and had some very terse words, with a few fisticuffs thrown in for good measure. My father wasn't having his daughter go back to work there!

Being female in education was not an issue, as 70 per cent of teachers are women. However, this is different in the principal class, where only 30 per cent of leaders are women. It was a pity that in the early days of education a woman had to pursue traditionally male knowledge, skills and actions to compete. I could ride a operate a motor mower, and every Friday I mowed the tee ball and softball pitches on the oval. I could activate and deactivate the alarm system, turn the heating system on and off, and relight the pilot light. I knew where the gas, electricity and water mains were in the school. I could get on the roof and retrieve the balls, put my hand down the toilet and unblock it, capture a dog in the yard, run a suspected robber out of the school, fix a leak, change the fuse in the electrical board, mend a leaking pipe, secure broken windows with shutters and cut down trees using an electric chainsaw. I could even drive a bus.

Having proved my prowess, I was slowly but surely accepted into the male realm of leadership. It was like a rite of passage. It is unfortunate that a woman who wanted to go up the ladder had to prove herself, but the long-term result was that it opened a lot of opportunities for me. Interestingly, it was sometimes the women on interview panels who needed the most convincing. I could demonstrate to the men that I could lead a school and do it well, but women would often see my bold, brazen prowess as aggressive. In my mind I was being assertive, showing my abilities and demonstrating leadership capabilities. Even when it took me 14 interviews to secure my first principal role, I was never defeated. I picked myself up, sought feedback on how I could do better and went around again. Finally in 2006 I became principal of the largest primary school in Victoria!

WONDER MOMENTS

These are the moments that you can see and feel, the moments that every teacher waits for. Moments like this sustained my passion for education over 46 years. When a student gets it, when the penny drops with their learning, you will realise the joy of teaching. You can see it in their eyes and their expressions. It is a magic moment and one that should be savoured.

CROSSING THINGS OFF YOUR LIST

As we grow older, our personal and professional roles change. Schools now need to prepare students to take on at least five different jobs. I met my husband when I was only 19 and married at 21, in the same year that I began teaching. Yes, yes, way too young, I know. I had my son at 24 and my daughter at 29. Each step up the career ladder was taken only after I considered the potential impact on my family. How were my long hours affecting them? How far would I have to drive each morning to drop my children off at childcare? What was the cost to our family harmony? I remember once writing an article for a magazine aimed at principals. I called it 'No Sex Please, I Am a New Principal!'. It was based on a survey of primary and secondary principals who revealed that their personal lives suffered because of their workload and hours. Our spouses went without. Could you believe that my article ended up being knocked back because the title was too risqué!

I would spend up to five years in each school learning as much as I could, taking on additional roles, stretching and challenging myself and learning. Then I would move on to another school for more seniority and responsibilities. The tougher the school, the more I learnt about student management and how to respond to difficult situations. I would look up to my leaders and watch what they did right and (more importantly) what they did wrong.

I applied for funding to run projects, I sought advice from my colleagues, and I asked lots and lots of questions. I would speak to the experts and ask them to show me how things were done. How did they file their school documents? I would ask them to come out to my school and show me how to set up my office and systems. I wasn't going to pretend I knew everything. A new principal has so much to learn. We have so many hopes and dreams for our school, but we first must tidy up any baggage left by the previous principal.

I was lucky with my first principalship. The school embraced me as their new leader and supported the changes that I recommended. We went from near closure to a blossoming student body after only six years. Our learning outcomes went from bad to outstanding. It was a school community that valued education and supported the teachers and leadership team.

My second principalship was more challenging. It was very multicultural, the largest government school in Victoria. There were more than 1000 students, 100 staff and 800 families. Only two or three staff in the school knew of me. As far as the rest were concerned, who was this new principal called Deborah Patterson? My introduction to the staff was icy and strained. The leadership team was divided and wary of me. I was told that the previous principal had stayed in her office while the staff ran the school! In my interview for the position, I had said to the selection panel that I would take my time, learn how things were done and not introduce anything too soon. That turned out to be wishful thinking. I learnt very little; walls were put up by some staff and people told me nothing unless I asked. Twelve staff left when they realised things were going to change, so I had to look for new staff to fill the vacancies. I was going full steam ahead.

With plenty of funds in the bank, we started spending money according to need. I put up signs showing that there was a new principal. I repainted doors, line-marking and games on the concrete for students to play on, renamed the canteen 'Kids Café' and decluttered the corridors, staff lounge and library. I reintroduced whole-school assemblies and made them kid-friendly, brought back the house system and welcomed in parents. I introduced team chants and fun games into the assemblies and made the student leaders run the weekly event. I waited outside the school before and after school, talking to as many parents as I could. I wanted to be seen and heard.

I appointed a teacher to rewrite our school values, tweaked the student code of conduct and advertised these to the wider school community. I started making changes with the students, the parents and eventually the staff. Finally—and it took time, hard work, long hours and discussions—the leadership team started to change their mindset and accept the cultural change. Those who did not like me or where the school was heading left, and this allowed me to bring in staff who were aligned with the new direction of the school. I had my good days, and even some great days. But in those early years were some very, very bad days. I remember that era as the loneliest of my job. At times, I thought that my breast cancer might come back from all the stress and pressure that I was experiencing. But over time, the staff slowly began to accept me. They became polite and were no longer afraid to be nice to me. Living my values of perseverance, staying true to myself, being a role model and practicing honesty with integrity saved the day! It took me a good five or six years to turn the school around to a place where we all knew our purpose, vision, mission, values, acceptable behaviours and conflict resolution. In those years I truly valued the support and loyalty of my school council presidents and councillors, my business manager, the education and support staff, the teachers, the leaders and the assistant principals. My colleagues were fantastic supporters. Another word of advice: have an outlet for your anger. I played netball. This allowed me to go to a game and play hard and fast to get it all out of my system. I pitied my opponents.

YELLOW SUNFLOWERS

For some reason I have always had a fascination with the colour yellow. I was even born with jaundice and my skin was a yellowish shade. Sickly or sunny? I lean toward the sunny side and believe that yellow symbolises sun, warmth and light. Yellow has pervaded my life. It is invigorating and stimulates our nerves, glands and brain, making us more alert and energised. Yellow boosts our memory and encourages communication. It is a colour that promotes enjoyment, activity and interaction.

As you might imagine, I'm a real fan of sunflowers—what better symbol of joy! When I was 12 years old, my father returned from a naval exercise with some gifts. He brought me a book of famous paintings. I treasured that book, and my favourite painting was one of Vincent van Gogh's sunflowers.

I saw those sunflowers at the National Gallery of Australia's van Gogh exhibition in April 2021 with my granddaughters Leah and Sarah. It was one of the highlights of my life. The sunflower has many meanings across the world. For me it means positivity, strength, admiration and loyalty. In Chinese culture, sunflowers are said to symbolise good luck and lasting happiness. They are often given out at graduations and at the start of a new business. Having sunflowers around my office and home brings joy and meaning to my day. What visual images do you have around you that bring you positivity and happiness?

I remember reading that flowers in a workplace improve productivity and positivity, and can also lower blood pressure and reduce stress and absenteeism. In a school, they add colour and create a welcoming environment for new parents, students and staff. Fresh plants and flowers in a work environment lift the mood, improve creativity and memory, and promote concentration.

When I obtained my first principal position, I spent three months painting and replacing display boards with colour. In my second school the colours were very corporate, so I replaced them with bolder and brighter colours. I spent a lot of money painting the concrete with colourful animals and games for the students to play during their recess and lunch breaks. I painted the entrance of all the external doors orange to promote happiness. It worked!

How you arrange the furniture in your office, classroom, boardroom or home can encourage positive energy. Schools and offices need airflow that is unrestricted by blockages and poor design. Positivity and creativity increase when energy is high. Colour, energy flow and natural sunlight play a significant role in effective design.

ZONES

When we know what is expected of us at work, we can fulfil our expected role and responsibilities. If you do not know what is expected of you, then find out. Staying in one's zone is the safest way to start any new position. Find out what is expected of you, seek clarity (in dot points if needed) and role descriptions. When you are unsure, ask for support or clarification. Flying blind is not recommended. You might think that you are doing the right thing, but you never know what will happen. On some occasions your contract might not be renewed. Being blindsided with an investigation or a complaint made against you is the very worst feeling. Stay true to your values and keep out of gossip, illicit relationships and petty arguments. Seek regular formal and informal feedback.

When should you venture outside your zone? Perhaps when you are planning and implementing your curriculum and assessment. All too often, I see teachers keep their eyes focused solely on the year level or faculty that they teach. Students achieve at levels above and below those typical for their grade. If you are unsure what to plan for a student or how to assess their work, go to your coordinator and get their support. All too often, teachers remain conservative and teach according to the year level of their students. You must plan and teach according to points of need. If you are not teaching to an accurate level, you cannot assess at an accurate level. Go outside your zone to cater for these students. Staying safe, being conservative and teaching within your comfort zone limits possibilities and opportunities for students who desperately need to work within their zone of proximal development. Push yourself, because every single student in your class deserves the best education you can provide for them.

ZZZ... SLEEP AND SYNC

When I was working full-time as the principal of one of the largest primary schools in Victoria, I woke at 6am and went to bed at 10pm every night. My headspace was always consumed with my profession. There was little room for personal or family issues. All I could think about was which meeting I had been in or was going to attend. I was constantly dealing with problems, troubleshooting and mediating disputes, arguments and inappropriate behaviour. I was a fixer, a doer and a judge. I lived this daily routine religiously for 22 years. When I eventually did get to sleep, I woke around 3am or 5am. No wonder I got sick and had breast cancer in 2002, a tumour on my thyroid in late 2016 and a stroke in 2019. My body was not getting the sleep it needed, nor did I have time to exercise. I was a walking timebomb!

Most adults need about eight hours of sleep per night. Children and teenagers need more sleep than adults, while older people tend to sleep more lightly and for shorter time spans than when they were younger. Unfortunately, when we work our headspace is filled with thoughts relating to our job. If we wake at 6am and go to bed at 10pm, that leaves eight hours for our bodies to refresh, recharge and reset for the following day. All too often many of us wake up in the early hours of the morning and cannot go back to sleep. We need to wake up feeling refreshed, energised for all the tasks ahead. A clear head allows us to make better decisions.

Getting enough sleep coordinates your head, inner core and limbs. As principal I was pulling 16-hour days and working on weekends as well. Listen to your body, rest, exercise and live well. Balance your routines and stay in control. Have regular health check-ups, meditate, read, walk daily and enjoy life outside your workplace. Spending time with family and loved ones increases the balance in your 'feel-good' bank. When you put in longer hours at work, you need to pay back or counterbalance that time with your home life for a better balance. We are not machines, so do not behave like one.

CONCLUSION

I knew in my second year of teaching that I wanted to be a leader. My team leader had done something wrong, and we were both asked to report to the principal's office. The principal asked a question and my team leader openly lied. What was worse, she looked at me and expected me to back her up. I did not, of course, but I wore the consequences from her for many years. It was then that I decided to upskill my knowledge and qualifications so that I could be a leader as someone who lived the values of honesty and integrity.

To be able to lead, teach and inspire others you have to be the best possible version of yourself. I wanted not only to act with integrity and honesty, but to improve student learning outcomes. I had to focus on my teaching craft, content and delivery, student management and interactions with others. I read widely, paid to attend professional development sessions and courses on weekends, and sought feedback from inspiring role models and mentors. I set high expectations and challenging goals and targets for myself and the students in my care. I looked for leadership opportunities to grow and develop within the education system.

When I thought that I was ready, I approached my principal to see if I could organise a whole-school event. It helped that I was his daughter's netball coach and they had recently won their grand final. He said yes! A principal allowing a second-year graduate teacher with little experience to plan, implement and run such an event in a school of over 500 students was a huge vote of confidence. He saw something in me and allowed me to take a risk! I never forgot how this made me feel, and as a principal I always encouraged my staff to take on opportunities so that they could grow and develop their leadership capabilities.

With success comes confidence. At the end of my second year, I was awarded a leadership mark indicating my responsibility, something that normally took 5-10 years to get. It was the beginning of my educational leadership journey, and I never looked back. When you love what you do, you are always learning along the way. When you feel valued in your growth as a leader, you are invested to do more.

To lead effectively is no simple feat, and the position of a principal can be a lonely one at times. If you use the right tools, tips and strategies to build your leadership capabilities and those of others around you, then everyone will benefit. Principals are now encouraged to be collaborative, communicate with others and share the load.

If you take one message from this book, let it be to never sacrifice your own health and wellbeing for any leadership aspiration. Life and work are about balance and momentum. Be gutsy, be passionate, take calculated risks, think creatively, plan strategically, do your due diligence, stay flexible, have respectful relationships and ride the leadership rollercoaster. But above all, listen to your body and be kinder to yourself. In the end, you will overcome the umpteen challenges to build clarity and change in your personal and professional life!

www.ingramcontent.com/pod-product-compliance
Lightning Source LLC
Chambersburg PA
CBHW050417120526
44590CB00015B/2004